A Path of Purpose

The Power of Focused Support and Targeted Care

Sharlene Meakins, BSN, RN

Shar Meakins, RN

authorHOUSE

AuthorHouse™
1663 Liberty Drive
Bloomington, IN 47403
www.authorhouse.com
Phone: 833-262-8899

© 2021 Sharlene Meakins, BSN, RN. All rights reserved.

No part of this book may be reproduced, stored in a retrieval system, or transmitted by any means without the written permission of the author.

Published by AuthorHouse   12/14/2020

ISBN: 978-1-6655-1051-6 (sc)
ISBN: 978-1-6655-1050-9 (hc)
ISBN: 978-1-6655-1052-3 (e)

Library of Congress Control Number: 2020924863

Print information available on the last page.

Any people depicted in stock imagery provided by Getty Images are models, and such images are being used for illustrative purposes only.
Certain stock imagery © Getty Images.

This book is printed on acid-free paper.

Because of the dynamic nature of the Internet, any web addresses or links contained in this book may have changed since publication and may no longer be valid. The views expressed in this work are solely those of the author and do not necessarily reflect the views of the publisher, and the publisher hereby disclaims any responsibility for them.

Contents

Foreword vii
Introduction xi

Chapter 1   Nursing School a Reality 1
Chapter 2   Anticipation of a New Career 7
Chapter 3   A Nurse is a Nurse is a Nurse...Right? 15
Chapter 4   A Desire to Make a Difference 19
Chapter 5   A Journey of Faith 23
Chapter 6   A New Me 27
Chapter 7   A Turn in the Journey 31
Chapter 8   The Learning Curve 39
Chapter 9   Communication and Building Trust 47
Chapter 10   Recognizing Value 57
Chapter 11   The Value of Implementing Professional Insight 63
Chapter 12   Mentoring to Make a Difference 67
Chapter 13   Facing the Unexpected 71
Chapter 14   Direct Support Professionals are Our Heros 79
Chapter 15   A Paper Trail and Data Review 87
Chapter 16   Continue to Grow And Invest in Yourself 91
Chapter 17   Perception is Everything 95
Chapter 18   Overcoming Trauma 101

Chapter 19   Wellness Vs Illness 105
Chapter 20   Healthcare Outside the DD Community 109
Chapter 21   The DD Nurse and the I/DD Provider 113

Final Thoughts 119
Acknowledgments 121
Glossary 123

Foreword

It is a warm September day in 1984. A faculty member asks an auditorium full of new baccalaureate nursing students, "Who is going to practice in the hospital after graduation?"

I was the only student who did not raise her hand. As an older returning student with a number of health education undergraduate courses under my belt, I had entered nursing school possessing a novice understanding of the multitude of factors that impact one's health and health behaviors. My 23-year-old brain at the time was thinking, *What better way to promote health and wellness than through the practice of nursing, but not in a hospital?* That turned out to be one of my best life decisions made at any age.

My first developmental disabilities nursing practice experience was with the state Office of Developmental Disabilities Services (ODDS). I practiced on a four-person team that traveled throughout the State of Oregon. We evaluated health-related services provided to adults with intellectual and developmental disabilities who received services in state and private Intermediate Care Facilities for Persons with Mental Retardation (ICF/MR). This was the late 1980's and the number of people living in these facilities was in the thousands.

I took pride in personally meeting and engaging with each person whose health and habilitative records I accessed. While my records evaluation targeted specific documents required for ICF/MR level services by the Code of Federal Regulation, I always made it a point to access and read each person's admission summary – some of which were frayed and yellowed with age having been held in the person's paper health record for well over 70 years.

My collection, validation of the synthesis of such data, allowed me to draw conclusions regarding the person's responses to their actual and potential health risks. Even as a relatively new RN, I began to recognize patterns of factors that affected peoples' risks. In addition to the origin of their developmental/intellectual disability and other medical/psychiatric diagnoses, the top contenders included:

- the person's method of communication
- the communication practices of staff responsible for the person's care
- the person's physical environment
- the person's social environment and relationships with others
- the competencies of individual medical professionals and staff assigned to provide the person's health and habilitative supports
- the practice competencies of individual RN to whom the person was assigned

And thus began my passion for DD Nursing practice.

Within the next 12 years, these facilities would all close. People were transitioned into private homes, foster homes, and congregate living situations. My nursing practice transitioned as well. The state-level regulatory evaluation of people's health and habilitative supports now took place with the community agencies that were providing residential and employment services to the former facility residents.

It was during my practice with ODDS that I became a Certified Developmental Disabilities Nurse. I started the Greater Oregon Nurse Associated with Development Disabilities (a local chapter of the Development Disabilities Nursing Association) and provided continuing education events for nurses practicing in the field of DD.

It was also during this time that I had the good fortune to meet

Sharlene Meakins. While Shar was a relatively new RN when we first met, I found her application of nursing science and ethical principle within her DD Nursing practice to be head and shoulders above the rest.

From 2002 forward, my nursing practice journey ventured on a different route. I took a practice position with Oregon's state office for seniors and then taught at Oregon Health & Science University School of Nursing. With no teaching responsibilities in the summer months, I opened an independent RN consulting business. For the past seven years, my practice is in nursing regulation at the Oregon State Board of Nursing.

To this day, Shar and I interact professionally and she has become a trusted colleague and friend. Every day I express gratitude for experiencing the most perfect nursing practice journey and gratitude for colleagues like Shar Meakins who have profoundly contributed to my journey and to the profession of nursing.

Gretchen Koch, MSN, RN
Policy Analyst at Oregon State Board of Nursing

Introduction

*"When you are a nurse, you know that every day you will touch
a life or a life will touch yours."*
- Anonymous

How often have you heard the question, "Which hospital or clinic do you work at?"

People often misunderstand the work of a community nurse. Their concept of a nurse is someone who gives injections, takes vitals, and administers medications. However, we are often behind the scenes traveling to individual's homes where we utilize our observation and assessment skills daily. We determine the needs of each patient which includes much-needed staff observations to be able to assess their health, activities of daily living support, and environment.

We as nurses, serve as an essential part of an individual's health care team to help facilitate life with health and wellness. We evaluate data and read progress notes to monitor for any signs or symptoms of change in an individual's health status. We not only complete documentation for assessments, care plans, protocols, and nursing orders, we also teach, train, and serve as an ally to professionally support each individual. As community nurses, we apply our nursing skills and scope of practice to individuals with a broad list of diagnoses, skill levels, and health needs.

By picking up this book, you represent someone who has the heart to follow *A Path of Purpose* with a passion to provide focused support and targeted care of others. My desire as you read about my personal journey is that you gain insight and direction for your own life and career. For chapter by chapter notes you can go to sharlenemeakins.com/resources to download journal pages for your own convenience. Whether you've just started as a new nurse, or have been a nurse or caregiver for several years, you will find it beneficial to reflect on your own journey and make course corrections where needed.

I recommend underlining, writing in the margins, and even journaling thoughts and ideas that come to you as you move forward in seeking and fulfilling your own purpose. Each of our journeys is exciting and unique just like the individuals we serve. My hope is that each of our lives is a reflection of love, kindness, joy, and peace as we walk in confidence and boldness to make a difference.

I decided to write this book because I wanted to make a broader impact in the Intellectual and Developmental Disabilities (I/DD) community. Often, as a new DD Nurse, I felt alone and had difficulty getting my footing since my expectations as an RN were different than what I was experiencing. I not only want to connect with my fellow DD Nurses but also encourage any of you who are feeling the calling to step out and start a service that would support the DD Community. I can honestly say from what I have experienced and observed, many who have started in this field have found their own path of purpose in serving individuals with developmental disabilities. The courage, strength, and love for life these individuals impart brings a new perspective to life.

I began to wonder, what have I learned and what can I impart to nurses inside and outside of the I/DD community? I would want to share my years of experience and understanding of:

1. How to communicate, listen, and observe individuals with I/DD
2. How to be a key player as a member of the individual support plan team
3. How to be an ally for an individual with I/DD

4. How to communicate with healthcare and mental health providers
5. How to develop a good working relationship with the staff
6. How to implement creative measures to implement a healthy lifestyle
7. How to provide dignity, respect, and independence

You may be someone who has been a caregiver for years as a parent, certified nurse assistant (CNA), personal support worker (PSW), or direct support professional (DSP). Maybe you manage a foster home, group home, or assisted living facility. Do you want to become a licensed practical nurse, registered nurse, or are you someone who is contemplating a change in their career?

Within these pages, my hope is to inspire you to move forward in pursuing your own goals and dreams. As you begin to read and apply my ideas, my desire is that you become passionate about your service and care for those you support. It's time to leave your past discouragements and failures behind and take the next step, whatever that may look like for you. No matter where we are on our journey, we can *make a difference together* as we use our gifts to learn and grow.

Visit my website sharlenemeakins.com to learn more about the training package I created for a New Developmental Disabilities Nurse.

Chapter One

NURSING SCHOOL A REALITY

"Don't let fear stop you, because if you do, you will miss AMAZING OPPORTUNITIES God has for YOU."
- Joyce Meyer

I recall the first week of class like it was yesterday. The instructor stood at the front of the classroom and said, "Look around at the other people in this room. At the end of the next 18 months, only half of you will graduate."

What? Really? I had no idea how challenging this journey to becoming a registered nurse would be. She said, "I don't want you to become a *refrigerator nurse*." We asked her what she meant. The instructor answered, "It's a nurse who only wants to make money so they can buy a refrigerator." She went on to explain that being a nurse requires a heart of compassion and caring.

I quickly connected with other students, who were closer to my children's ages than my own, but we built good relationships. The students were supportive and we often spent time studying together to improve our success. Boy, were these 'kids' smart! I often found myself intimidated by their intellect but I moved forward knowing that God would give me the strength and understanding I needed to complete my degree. Needless to say, I did sweat over a test or two to be able to maintain at least a B average. If you didn't maintain a B average, you would be dismissed from the nursing program.

As a non-traditional student (and a grandma in my case), I knew that I needed to take advantage of every tutor and study group I could connect with. I was so grateful for the tutors who could explain concepts to me in ways that I would understand. I began to realize that my years of experience and connections helped lay the foundation for me to become a registered nurse.

After several months, immense hours of studying and late nights completing assignments, the time had come for our class to begin clinicals. It was true, almost half of the students had already either dropped out or were dismissed from the nursing program. I was always in awe of the remaining students that were parents and did their best to take care of their young families and remain in the nursing program. I remembered how difficult it was for our family when I was attending night classes years before.

On the first morning of clinicals, I stood looking at my reflection in the mirror. I had neatly pressed my student nurse's uniform and bought a new pair of white comfortable shoes. I sensed God speaking to my heart, "This is My gift of joy to you." Tears filled my eyes. I knew I would love being a nurse and it would give me great joy. I was overwhelmed with the anticipation of graduating from college and actually receiving an Associate Degree in Nursing.

For the next six months, I began applying my knowledge to what I had learned in the classroom. I thoroughly enjoyed the opportunities I had to work in long-term care, memory care, pediatrics, labor & delivery, an emergency department, mental health, out-patient surgery, and community health for young mothers and their babies. Despite the fact that a few of us were carpooling at 4:30 a.m. to drive to our clinical location, we looked forward to the clinical experiences. My preceptors were so supportive and encouraging. I particularly enjoyed outpatient surgery.

Finally, the 'Big Day' arrived. The nurses pinning ceremony was about to begin. My husband, who supported me and encouraged me each step of the way, was beaming as he walked up to the front of the auditorium to apply my nurse's pin.

After the graduation ceremony, the end of the day brought sweet sorrow among the students. We knew we would be going our separate ways. We were saying our goodbyes after spending almost two years together day-in and day-out throughout the grind of the nursing program.

Over the next several weeks, each one of us would be scheduling our NCLEX-RN exam so we could acquire our license to practice nursing. I took mine within the following two weeks. I knew if I put it off, I would grow exceedingly nervous and fearful. So I took the plunge and got it behind me as quickly as possible.

The exam measured your ability to problem solve and determine the best answer for each scenario. Often each answer was correct but you had to choose which answer was the *first* action step you would take. I walked out of the exam after two hours feeling hopeless. *Would I pass?* I had to wait several days to receive my results. I was both elated and relieved to learn I had passed!

LISA'S STORY

From day one, I sat in the front row of the classroom. The opening statement my teacher said was, "Most of you won't make it to the end and graduate."

Stunned, I immediately stole a glance at those around me and noticed a wide range of people. I saw men and women, old and young. Some were moms, dads, and even grandmas. *Who wasn't going to make it? Would it be me?* I knew I was extremely focused and a hard worker. I was determined to keep going until I had the RN credentials after my name.

I decided to join study groups. That's where I met Shar.

I remember our first conversation like it was yesterday. We discovered we lived in the same apartment complex right next to the school. She had grandkids that were around the same age as my son. Little did Shar know but I had been praying for someone like her to come into my life. I was homesick, scared and I didn't know anyone. We had moved from Washington to Idaho so I could go to nursing school. I was just getting settled into our new place.

As time went on, I developed a close friendship with Shar and I knew God had placed her so perfectly in my life to help me through this journey. Shar and her husband quickly took us under their wings. Whether it was long talks, dinners, or going for a walk they became our family and lifelong friends.

Nursing school was now my all-consuming focus. Every quarter I gave a huge sigh of relief that I had completed one more. I quickly developed a routine to accomplish my goals. A lot of sweat and tears went into every exam that moved me into the next quarter and closer to becoming an RN.

On the very last day of school, I remember looking around to see who all made it. Out of my entire cohort, only two of us were part of our original class. What I learned at that moment wasn't about who had made it, but recognizing it was about all the life lessons that happened along the way. Nursing school was character building. God had used this experience to shape me into the nurse and woman He wanted me to be. I looked around the room one more time and realized my journey was just beginning.

Lessons Learned:

- Pursuing a career may be a difficult uphill climb but remember it is worth it when you reach a life of joy and fulfillment at the top.
- Our years of experience are not in vain, but rather they form the foundation that we build upon as we follow our life path.
- Learning and growing together gives strength and courage to keep moving forward.

Chapter Two

ANTICIPATION OF A NEW CAREER

*"The whole secret of a successful life
is to find out what is one's destiny to do, and then do it."*
~ Henry Ford

During my last four months of nursing school, my daughter and her family (including our three granddaughters) moved out of state. As they contemplated their move, they recognized they did not want to keep us and our granddaughters apart and asked if we would also consider moving. Since I would be graduating soon, we were free to go anywhere we wanted next. In order to be near our granddaughters, we packed up and moved in with our daughter and her family after graduation and stayed with them for the next six months.

I wasn't able to begin searching for a nursing job until I had received a license for the State of Oregon. I submitted my Board of Nursing application which would take several weeks to be approved. Meanwhile, I went to a job service to apply for a temporary job. An agency that managed adult group homes hired me as a direct support professional (DSP) providing care for individuals with intellectual and developmental disabilities (I/DD). I had never been in a group home for individuals with I/DD and realized how much I enjoyed this job and inquired about working as a nurse for the agency, with no response.

I received my license within the next two months and began my search for an out-patient surgery position for which I had references from my preceptors. I submitted application after application with no success. The local hospital told me they were hiring RNs with a baccalaureate degree in nursing (an RN with a four-year college or university degree). I couldn't believe it! I had just spent the last six years going to school and I couldn't even work at the local hospital! So my search continued.

A surgical center called me back for a second interview but I was ultimately not hired because another applicant had more experience. I didn't know where to turn but soon found a per diem position to provide in-home nursing care for children with intellectual and developmental disabilities. I took the position even though I wasn't promised full-time hours, or given benefits. But at least I could start working.

I had the opportunity to support a mother on the graveyard shift and her toddler son. I thoroughly enjoyed providing care for the toddler who required 24-hour nursing services that involved oxygen monitoring and trachea care. I had never known anyone who had nursing services for their child at home. This opened a new awareness for me.

A short time later, my daughter found a job as a personal support worker (PSW) caring for a child through the State Department of Human Services. I also became involved in this family's life by applying to be their delegation RN when the previous RN was moving out of the area. Their child required nursing care as well as PSWs to provide support for them and their family. It became obvious how skilled my daughter and the other staff were in providing care for this beautiful child who had a high level of medical needs. I had the responsibility of completing an assessment, writing a care plan, and health-related protocols, along with the training, assignment, and delegation of the PSWs.

However, this was again an independent side job that I was doing to support the family and offered no health insurance benefits. Even though I was enjoying the nursing care I was providing, as the new year turned the corner I found myself discouraged because I had not yet found a full-time position that offered benefits.

The annual *20 Days of Prayer and Fasting* was starting the next day at church and I recall praying, *"Lord, you are the one that tapped me on the shoulder to go back to college to get my nursing degree, so I know you have the perfect nursing position for me. I'm not going to apply for another nursing job during this time of prayer and fasting. I am going to believe You to direct me to the right position for me."*

Once again, the Lord was allowing me the opportunity to depend on Him rather than on myself. The next day, a woman from the temporary job service I had used when I first moved to town three months earlier, called me and asked, "Shar, have you gotten a full-time nursing position yet?"

I said, "No, I've been working per diem without benefits."

"Well," she said, "this agency, similar to the one you were a DSP for adults with I/DD, has called me looking for an RN. They have never called me before and you were the first one I thought of. Would you like to come in for an interview tomorrow?"

Of course, I said yes. I couldn't believe the Lord would bring an opportunity to me so quickly.

The next day, I went to the interview and met the woman who was in charge of HR and a gentleman who was the new executive director. As we visited, they asked me questions about writing care plans and doing assessments which is standard during RN clinicals. But, the question that got my attention the most was, "Why do you want to be a DD Nurse?"

I smiled and said, "I didn't know that I did."

The director went on to ask, "Well, what kind of experience have you had with individuals with I/DD?"

All of a sudden, it was as if the Lord put a movie trailer in front of me that showed all the people throughout my life who had disabilities. I recalled as a grade-schooler, a young man at church with Down Syndrome that loved my dad and a blonde teenage girl that had a wheelchair. I also recalled friends and neighbors who had family members with disabilities that I knew and provided respite for.

One such friend and her sister with cerebral palsy is a part of our family's wonderful connection to the DD community. Also, my husband and I were asked to provide respite for a gentleman in a foster home that we lived in the last four months of nursing school. Wow! I had no idea that I had so much experience supporting families and individuals with intellectual and developmental disabilities!

In astonishment, I looked at the director and said, "I guess I've had a lot of experience."

I had no idea that this wasn't the norm for someone to have multiple relationships with individuals who have I/DD.

As the interview was drawing to a close, I explained that my husband and I had been working together for 25+ years for non-profit organizations. Our experience varied from caring for the homeless, having a food bank in our basement, and being houseparents for foster children in a group home, so I was very familiar with working for a non-profit. I was offered the position as an RN for the agency that would shortly work into a full-time position with benefits.

Back in my car, I started worshipping! All the way home, I just kept praising the Lord for opening the door for the perfect nursing position. I was filled with gratitude as I realized He had been just waiting for me to trust Him.

After arriving home, my husband asked me what I had said. I explained that I had told the director that we had worked together for non-profit agencies most of our marriage and that we were a good team in caring for people. My husband then shared that the HR director had called and offered him a job as a caregiver. Not only had the Lord directed my steps, but He also had a plan for my husband as we began a new chapter in our lives caring for individuals with intellectual and developmental disabilities.

I called one of my nursing school instructors who had previously lived and worked in the area where I was now living to tell her about my new position as an I/DD Nurse and she was thrilled. She exclaimed, "Shar, that is a perfect career for you."

I had no idea that DD Nursing was a nursing career since I don't recall even discussing it as an option during nursing school.

The University of New Hampshire's 2019 Annual Report on People with Disabilities in America reports that 42,630,000 people are affected by disabilities. That means 13.1 percent of the population in the U.S. The majority of these individuals are living with families, but a quarter of them receive services through publicly funded programs such as Medicaid or Medicare. This means there is a real need for DD Nurses throughout the United States in order to support individuals, families, and staff with health and wellness supervision and intervention.

As a result of the lack of training for nurses to work in the I/DD field, I routinely see nurses and care staff that don't know how to support someone with I/DD. There are also community nurses who do not want to serve the I/DD population due to a personal fear of working with I/DD individuals, whether it be in private homes, foster homes, or group homes. It's my belief that nurse training needs to include clinicals in the I/DD community.

PAT'S STORY

Throughout my life, I have been asked, "Don't you wish your sister was "normal?"

My sister, Peggy, suffered a brain injury at birth because the labor and delivery nurse told our mother to not let the baby come until the doctor arrived. As her first year passed by, it was evident that Peggy had developmental delays. She was diagnosed with *cerebral palsy* caused by a lack of oxygen at birth. The doctor advised our parents that she should be 'institutionalized' because it was going to be difficult to raise her at home. He told my parents she wouldn't live to become an adult.

Dad told the doctor, "God gave us this child and we are going to raise her by His strength and guidance."

We grew up in rural South Dakota. Mom and Dad were married after Dad returned from WWII. Peggy was born three years later. I was born four years after Peggy, followed by three brothers. Mom had two sisters and a brother. Dad was an only child. We had the privilege of knowing both sets of grandparents. Our cousins on our mother's side were like siblings, as we gathered for every holiday, birthday, and anniversary that came along. We had support from this close-knit family who treated Peggy like anyone else.

Our parents found out that a school about 40 miles from our farm was going to offer a 'special education' class for children who were 'slow learners.' They decided to enroll Peggy. For the next several years, Mom would load up all the kids and drive to that school so Peggy could attend the class every morning, five days a week.

When I became old enough to attend grade school, Mom could no longer take Peggy to that school. But then a "special education" class became available in a town 10 miles in the other direction from where I attended school, so Peggy attended that class until she became too old.

Speech and language pathologists were not yet available. Peggy's speech was affected by the CP so it was hard to understand her at times. Because Peggy and I were so close, I learned how to interpret what she was saying. And she was really good at showing me pictures or objects to help me understand what she was trying to communicate.

We grew up. I got married and moved away a year after our mother died. But Dad continued to be adamant about taking care of Peggy with the same conviction he had when she was born. By that time, there was a home service available in the community that sent a lady to the farm once a week to provide personal care for Peggy, as well as housekeeping duties for Dad.

My husband was a manager with a large retail company who transferred us out of state. I was a medical transcriptionist and it was through my job at one of the local hospitals that I met Shar. Her warm smile and friendly personality drew me to her immediately. She invited us to their church and we became close friends. Our husbands also became friends. Shar mentored me, gently leading me and challenging me to grow in my faith.

When my Dad and Peggy would come to visit us, they would spend time with Shar and her family as well. It was during one of these visits that Shar spoke to Peggy about Jesus dying on the cross for her. We had attended church and Sunday School since we were little, but I had never asked Peggy if she believed. To this day, Peggy is quick to tell people that Jesus died for her and she will say, "Amen, Amen" for them as she folds her hands.

Do I wish my sister was 'normal?' All I can say is that Peggy has always loved me unconditionally. I have been truly blessed to have her in my life.

Lessons Learned:

- **Life leaves clues along our path that lead us to our destination; we may only recognize these clues when we look back from where we came.**
- **The people we connect with throughout our journey are not by happenstance; these individuals provide a new perspective and understanding to life.**
- **When new opportunities present themselves, explore them; they may be the very thing you were looking for.**

Chapter Three

A NURSE IS A NURSE IS A NURSE...RIGHT?

*"Sometimes I inspire my patients;
more often they inspire me."
~ Unknown*

Interestingly enough, most of us may think *a nurse is a nurse, is a nurse... right?* I have come to realize that each field of nursing is unique and requires different additional skill sets. Even though each nurse graduates with basic nursing knowledge and skills, it's not until you choose a field of nursing to work in that you begin to understand and experience the additional skills and knowledge required.

A developmental disability nurse first and foremost must serve as a part of an individual's support team to ensure that the individual's rights and values are recognized, respected, and upheld. A nurse must expand his or her knowledge and understanding of the particular diagnosis of an individual with intellectual or developmental disabilities has. As a DD Nurse, we must be familiar with the definitions of abuse and requirements of mandatory abuse reporting.

Abuse of an individual with developmental disabilities can range from accidental death, financial exploitation, and verbal mistreatment to placing restrictions on an individual's freedom of choice which includes movement. A nurse, or anyone that observes or even suspects abuse or neglect, is required to make an immediate phone call to the authorities. In light of supporting a vulnerable population, whether due to age or disability, it's important that we respond with integrity.

The nurse must have a holistic health practice that enables him or her to not only examine the body but also to recognize the needs and health of the mind and spirit. In addition, it is essential that the DD Nurse develops the ability to observe, listen, and draw from the individual's circle of influence that includes their family, friends, and caregivers.

A DD Nurse may be required to train an unlicensed person such as a direct support professional (DSP) to perform medical care tasks that would normally be performed by a nurse in a facility setting. The fact that many more individuals are living independently, or in foster or residential group homes, requires additional training for the caregivers.

In such cases where an individual may have a gastrostomy, a colostomy, trachea, or even need medication administered subcutaneously, an RN might be required to delegate a caregiver to perform the nursing task. As a result, it is the responsibility of the RN to not only to be skilled in the task at hand (or acquire the skill), but to also provide training, clear instruction (both verbal and written), and review the caregiver's skills performing the nursing task.

Nurses must not assume a level of experience, knowledge, and understanding when training support staff. The mistake I made early on in my career was not only assuming but delegating every and all staff for the nursing task. I came to find out that not only am I placing the individual at risk but my license at risk as well if I am not confident that the caregiver can perform the task correctly.

I assumed that all the staff needed to be trained but learned to be wise in staff choices for delegation. I began to recognize that not every DSP has a desire to perform a nursing task or have the thought process to thoroughly complete a nursing task. Therefore, it was important that I ensure that there was a competent staff person on duty who could and would perform the nursing task and call me with any questions or health concerns.

It is important that we build a team of support staff that take the nursing tasks seriously and are able to recognize the complications that could occur and what to do in an emergency. For this reason, accurate and detailed protocols must be written for staff to be able to identify signs and symptoms of complications for all health risks that are identified for an individual.

This brings up another point. Instructions need to be written for staff in a step-by-step process in simple or nonmedical terms. Often nurses use medical terms and language that make it difficult for a staff person to understand and follow. Also, as a side note, be aware of the primary language of a DSP. If all your instruction is written in English, and it's their second language, you need to verify that they understand what they have read. Don't assume that a smile and a nod of the head indicate understanding. Use written and oral quizzes along with asking the staff person to demonstrate the task to ensure they comprehend the instructions and protocol.

As a reminder for nurses and DSPs, follow any mandated administrative rule(s) written by the board of nursing around the delegation of nursing tasks to ensure the highest level of safety is implemented.

Lessons Learned:

- **Even though each nurse graduates with basic nursing knowledge and skills, it's not until you choose a field of nursing to work in that you begin to understand and experience the additional skills required.**

- Ensure that those to whom you are delegating tasks have the desire and competence to understand and perform those tasks along with skills that are typically performed by a nurse.
- Give clear instruction and training to the staff providing support for daily living activities that will produce success.

Chapter Four

A DESIRE TO MAKE A DIFFERENCE

"One person can make a difference, and everyone should try."
- John F. Kennedy

I believe each of us is born with a desire to make a difference in the world. I also believe that most of us have had our personal dreams and desires squelched - whether by our own negative self-talk or by the words of impossibility through others - maybe a parent, sibling, grandparent, or even a best friend.

I vividly remember the time as an elementary child when I wanted to make a difference. I had dreams, desires, and ambitions. I enjoyed going to Sunday School and church with my family. I grew up with grandparents, aunts, uncles, and cousins who all went to the same church. Believing in God was an important part of growing up. I remember as a little girl spending time with my grandmother. While sitting on her lap, she shared with me her favorite Psalm in the Bible: *Psalm 27*. She also told me her favorite hymn was *What A Friend We Have In Jesus*. I cherished my grandmother's love and those memories made a lifelong impression on me.

I desired to follow God and to please Him. I thought to follow God meant that I would be a missionary like my Dad's cousin, Juliet, who was a missionary overseas in Africa. When I was eight, my parents took me to listen to her presentation on her missionary work. This greatly stirred my young heart. During the presentation, I was enthralled with the slides and stories that were shared. When my parents and I got into the car to head home, I proclaimed to my Dad, "I want to be a missionary overseas just like your cousin!"

My proclamation was immediately followed by my dad's discouraging statement, "It's too dangerous to be a missionary in Africa!" He added that his cousin would agree. That was the first big blow to my desire to be a missionary.

Throughout my school years, I struggled academically. I convinced my parents to let me go to school at age four. I would be five in another month and I wanted to go to school with my cousin who was ten months older. Yes, the rebellious, oldest child in me raised its ugly head, not understanding learning developmental delays because of being born two months premature.

During the first four years of elementary school, my parents wanted to hold me back in order to give me an opportunity to improve my learning and comprehensive skills. But, once again, I insisted that I not be kept back because I didn't want to leave my school friends. The results weren't pretty.

The teachers did all they could to assist me. I remember staying in from recess at times to work extra with the teacher. I was also placed in a remedial reading class in order to improve my reading skills. They taught me to sit still and focus on comprehending what I was reading. I remained in that class until junior high school.

Time after time my attempts to do better failed. I allowed the negative words of others to dictate how I felt about myself. I was one of the least successful students in our small class of 36. As a freshman in high school, my Algebra teacher sent me to the school counselor to get moved out of Algebra. It was too difficult for me and I didn't need the class to graduate (not realizing at the time I was going to need it in college and nursing school).

I continued to barely pass my highschool classes - except I aced band, choir, typing class, and home economics. I compared myself to my peers based on what I could and couldn't do. I believed that I wasn't smart enough. I wasn't athletic enough. I wasn't pretty enough. I felt like I didn't belong and I began to settle for being '*less than*.'

As a senior in high school, I enjoyed my lifelong friends but I still didn't feel like I belonged. I didn't go out on the weekends to activities with my girlfriends because they all had boyfriends. As a result, I began making lifestyle decisions that I knew were not pleasing to God in order to feel like I belonged. My desire to make a difference in the world began to diminish.

My parents attempted to encourage me. They reassured me that even though I hadn't excelled in school, I would be a good wife and mother. Neither of my parents graduated from high school so they didn't want me to set my sights too high, only to fail. Thus, my desire as an independent, stubborn, firstborn was to live on my own and declare, "I know what's best for my life!" I often rebelled against my dad's instruction and concerns in the choices I was making.

I'm sure many of you have similar stories. Stories of rebellion for various reasons with feelings of hopelessness and settling for second, third, or even fourth-best rather than the purpose we were created to fulfill.

Life Lessons:

- **Don't live your life off someone else's script or experiences; we are each born with unique personalities, gifts, and strengths.**
- **Hold onto your childhood dreams and desires despite other people's fears; you may be the one to fill the gap for the next generation.**
- **Your childhood struggles do not need to dictate your adult academics with your desire to learn.**

Chapter Five

A JOURNEY OF FAITH

The thief comes only to steal and kill and destroy;
I came so that they would have life, and have it abundantly.
John 10:10 NASB

After high school, I moved away from home to attend community college. My nightlife and my friendships were more of a priority than my classes. My desire to belong continued to overshadow my heart's desire to please God. My lifestyle left me with guilt and shame. So after partying on Saturday night, I would get up every Sunday morning to attend church service. Despite my continued rebellion and moving out of the dormitory to live independently (which I can only assume was still on my dad's dime), I graduated with my diploma as a medical secretary.

I went on to start my first job as a secretary, but not a medical secretary. Again my performance, just as it had been as a student, was less than desirable. I continued to live an active nightlife. After a few months, my employer placed me on probation because I arrived at work late, most likely hungover. I didn't want to get fired, so I quit.

Remarkably, I was able to get a job for the city as a secretary in a small utility office. Nothing changed in my lifestyle but it was there I was faced with a staff who was different than anyone I had ever met. Because the office was outside of town, the five of us would bring a sack lunch. One of my coworkers would read his Bible while eating his chicken salad on rye. I had never before seen anyone read their Bible outside of church or home, but to Bob, it came naturally. I was intrigued, yet unsure whether I really wanted to get to know him. In fact, I was rather rude.

Despite my unkindness, Bob started a conversation with me during one of our lunch breaks.

He asked, "If you were to die tonight, do you know where you would go?"

What a strange question! No one had ever asked me that before. I pondered for a moment and said, "I guess I would go to heaven because I've never killed anyone."

Besides, I go to church and believe in God. Isn't that enough?

Bob patiently continued his questioning, "Do you believe in Jesus? Do you think you are a sinner?"

I had no doubt in my mind that I believed in Jesus. I had wonderful memories of going to church with my grandpa to make repairs and care for the cemetery grounds. I always enjoyed attending Sunday School and youth groups. However, I also had no doubt that I was a sinner because of my self-indulgent lifestyle. I was filled with guilt and shame.

Sensing my hesitation, Bob looked straight in my eyes and asked, "Do you believe Jesus died for your sins?"

"Yes...I think so."

I really wasn't sure that I would go to heaven to be with Him when I died.

As if reading my mind, Bob said, "But you can know."

"Really? You can know if you're going to heaven or not?"

Bob then explained to me that we each have a personal decision to make in our faith journey.

Believe that Jesus is the Son of God.
If you declare with your mouth, "Jesus is Lord," and believe in your heart that God raised him from the dead, you will be saved. Romans 10:9, NIV

Believe that Jesus died for my sins.
For God so loved the world that he gave his one and only Son, that whoever believes in him shall not perish but have eternal life. John 3:16, NIV

Confess my sin.
If we confess our sins, he is faithful and just and will forgive us our sins and purify us from all unrighteousness. I John 1:9, NIV

Believe that God has a plan for my life.
For I know the plans I have for you," declares the LORD, "plans to prosper you and not to harm you, plans to give you hope and a future. Jeremiah 29:11, NIV

Again, my deepest desire was to follow God and I knew that I wanted to be in heaven with Jesus when I died. That night when I got ready for bed, I did the only thing I knew to do. I knelt down next to my bed to pray:

"Jesus, I know that I'm a sinner. I believe that you died for my sins. Please come into my heart and take control of my life. I want to be in heaven with You when I die. Amen"

I got up from my knees, crawled into bed, and fell asleep satisfied that I would go to heaven when I died. The next day, Bob asked me if I had gone home and prayed. I said, yes, that I had prayed. Bob literally jumped for joy! At the time, I didn't fully comprehend his excitement, but I felt the assurance of my salvation. Little did I know that my faith journey with Jesus had just begun. My life was about to take a 180-degree turn and my desire to make a difference in the world soon resurfaced.

Sharlene Meakins, BSN, RN

Lessons Learned:

- We are each born with a purpose. Don't let your God-given dreams and desires die with you. Go for it!
- I could not place my trust in my parents' faith; I had to make a faith decision for myself.
- Faith is not a moment in time, but the beginning of a journey to grow into your purpose.

Chapter Six

A NEW ME

"Anything is possible when you have the right people there to support you."
~ Misty Copeland

After my new found relationship with Jesus, my life changed dramatically. I experienced a sudden passion for reading and studying the Bible. I began to dig deep and actually comprehend what I was reading. I lost my desire to go to the bar with friends after work. I no longer cared about doing things to fit in because I no longer needed their approval. I quit using filthy language and discontinued my self-indulgent lifestyle. My old way of life no longer held any appeal to me. I was literally a different person as described in 2 Corinthians 5:17 which says, *"Therefore, if anyone is in Christ, he is a new creation. The old has passed away; behold, the new has come."* ESV

My parents didn't understand my renewed desire to please God and follow His ways because I had always "believed in Jesus." My determination to make a difference in the world and be a missionary resurfaced and I started to grow in my faith and study the Word of God with other women. I did a word study on my name, the names of my parents, and the names of my grandparents. My name meant 'womanly' and I was intrigued that my grandmother's name meant 'nurse.' I still held the limiting belief that

I wasn't smart enough to be a nurse, but the desire was there in the back of my mind since I adored my grandmother.

My grandmother and I had always shared a special bond. I recall a time when I was in first or second grade. I didn't get on the bus after school as expected but instead walked the few blocks to go visit Grandma. The look of surprise on her face is to this day a precious memory! (My family lived on a farm next to my grandparent's original homestead eight miles outside of town.) After she got over her initial shock, my grandmother smiled and said that she had better call my mom to let her know that I had come for a visit. My mom wasn't very happy about having to come pick me up, but I was delighted to visit Grandma as I reached into the kitchen drawer that I knew was always supplied with packages of Cherry Nibs.

Years later, I was devastated to learn that when I was in high school, my dad's family had asked my parents if I could help take care of my grandmother at home. I would have loved the opportunity to help care for her! Apparently, however, my mom said "No" because she was jealous of my relationship with my dad's family. I was hurt that I hadn't even been asked and, therefore, deprived of caring for the woman who had first taught me about Jesus' love.

As a new follower of Jesus, I began to attend a small Baptist church where I learned about water baptism. My dad was not happy with me when I wanted to be baptized as an adult since I was baptized as a baby. But, as I read the Bible, I believed that Scripture teaches us to follow Jesus in water baptism.

At this Baptist church, I met a veterinarian and his wife who owned a small animal clinic. They invited me to come to work for them as their only full-time employee. I eagerly accepted their invitation since this was a far better fit for me. Not only was I able to use my medical secretary skills, but I also learned how to be a lab technician, x-ray technician, customer service provider, salesperson, and even at times...a janitor.

It was during this season of employment that my Christian bosses gently and lovingly taught me how to be a beneficial employee. They instructed me on how to set my priorities based on their needs and not follow my own ideas on what I thought was important. God used this experience to help me learn obedience and not follow my independent streak.

One day, my cousin's wife stopped by the clinic. She had brought with her a book titled, **Joni**. It was a true story about a young woman who, at the age of 17, had a life-altering accident. After diving into the Chesapeake Bay, she broke her neck leaving her a quadriplegic with the inability to care for herself. I eagerly read Joni's story and was amazed by her desire to live for Jesus despite the disappointments and challenges in her life. Joni's journey of faith has continued to intrigue me as she and her husband went on to develop an amazing ministry called, *Joni and Friends*. Their Mission Statement is: *To glorify God as we communicate the Gospel and mobilize the global church to evangelize, disciple, and serve people living with disabilities.* You can go to https://www.joniandfriends.org/ to learn more.

As I reflect back now on those three years of employment at the veterinary clinic, I recall two gentlemen with mental challenges who would come into the clinic with their small dogs. I realize that the Lord was teaching me even then how to build relationships with individuals who had intellectual and developmental disabilities. I enjoyed getting to know each of them as they would each stop in often to say 'hi' even if their pet didn't have an appointment. In fact, when I became engaged to be married, both men told me that they needed to meet my future husband to approve of him before we got married. I made sure they did.

I eventually moved on to working as a medical secretary with a non-profit medical clinic for two physicians I had met at church. My housemate also worked there. I was delighted to be working at a clinic for people, but I'll never forget the life lessons I learned at the veterinary clinic. My husband often joked that I knew everyone and their dog in town.

During my employment at the medical clinic, I had the opportunity to experience the different aspects of the clinic from the front office as a receptionist, to transcription, and then onto becoming a medical assistant. My love for the medical community grew. Much to my amazement, co-workers, nurses, and physicians began to tell me that I would make a good nurse. I again proclaimed to myself and others that I wasn't smart enough to be a nurse. However, Sharon, an RN at the clinic, listened to my story of academic failure, and not only offered ongoing encouragement, but she also offered to tutor me. As a result of her support and many others, I made the decision to go back to the community college I had previously attended. I signed up for night classes in order to complete the prerequisites for applying to a nursing program. Trudy spent long hours with me, helping me grasp the now required algebra assignments. And she continued to faithfully tutor me along my entire college pathway.

During this time, we had a son born with physical defects. Looking back, I also find it interesting that God was preparing me for a career as a DD Nurse even then. In addition to our son, we also had neighbors and friends with children and family members that had intellectual and developmental disabilities. My family and I would often support these families by providing respite care for a few hours. These times became some of our fondest memories and friendships as a family.

Lessons Learned:

- **Believe in yourselves and do not listen to the lies that scroll through your mind. It's never too late to overcome those lies and move forward on your path of purpose.**
- **The value of being a good employee includes listening to your employer's instructions; do not lean on your own understanding. Be teachable.**
- **It's important to ask questions. Too often we are only looking through our limited understanding.**

Chapter Seven

A TURN IN THE JOURNEY

"If you do what you love, you'll never work a day in your life."
- Marc Anthony

In order for me to go to night classes part-time, my husband would come home from work and need to care for our five children, ages ten, eight, six, five, and three. After two semesters into college, we had the opportunity to go to work for a newly opened rescue mission for the homeless. Meanwhile, my husband became an ordained pastor and served as the discipleship pastor for the men who came to the shelter with a desire to grow in their faith. Because I mistakenly thought that following God meant that I needed to be working in ministry, I decided to leave the medical clinic and serve as administrative assistant to the mission's director.

One day the mission's executive director asked me why I wanted to continue going to college to be a nurse when I was already in full-time ministry. Because my schedule was packed full with raising five children while assisting to run not only a men's homeless shelter, but we were also now opening a new women's and family shelter, I resigned myself to the belief that others knew what was best for me. I decided not to return to school the following semester and I stopped pursuing my education to become a nurse.

The next two years of ministry were successful at the men's, women's, and family shelters. I had learned to provide support to the ministry and create promotional materials to the local churches and community. However, I began to notice that the director wasn't pleased with my husband's performance since they had different perspectives on ministering styles. Regrettably, I now realize that I was concerned about my husband experiencing rejection in a career that he enjoyed. I began to carry the responsibility for his happiness which was not mine to carry.

Little did I know there was another upcoming fork in the road of our journey. We were offered an opportunity to work for another rescue mission for the homeless in a different state. *Move out of state?* I reasoned it would be closer to my husband's family. I had never moved further than 40 miles from my childhood home since going to community college at 17. We took the plunge and moved our family 1200 miles literally due west on Highway 20.

Shortly after our arrival, my husband heard that an area Christian college was starting a nursing program and asked if I would like to go back to finish my nursing degree. My interest was stirred, but I didn't feel comfortable leaving our now 16, 14, 12, 11, and soon-to-be 9-year-old at home alone after school in a new community while I was at classes. Instead, I went to work at the main office of the rescue mission 30 miles from our home. I soon learned that I didn't like commuting to the city for work. Especially when my children would get sick at school, it was difficult to run home to care for them. As a result, much to the disappointment of the rescue mission administration, I resigned.

I found employment through a woman I met at our new church. This time, I worked for the school district only three short blocks from our home. The training I'd received learning computer skills at the medical clinic really paid off. At the time, I had falsely believed that I could never learn to use a computer because when I attended community college years before, a computer was the size of a room! So, when I was introduced to a desktop computer to type transcription at the medical clinic, I was so scared that I began to cry. However, due to a patient and kind RN at the medical clinic, I overcame my fear, and working on a computer became an avenue of skill and gratification.

I was enjoying my employment at the school district, but one year after uprooting our family and moving west, far from our extended family and friends, the director of this new mission announced that he was returning to the mission in the midwest. The following year a new director was hired and my husband was asked to resign. The job that my husband had a great passion for was snatched out from under him. He slid back into depression and despair.

After two years, he still had not found full-time employment. I still was under the belief that I needed to make sure he was happy, so I applied for a job for us both to be live-in house parents for a children's group foster home. There was room for our own four children (the oldest was now out of the house) plus eight foster children. We were once again working for a non-profit ministry.

The home had been built and established by a local church and a couple who had a heart for foster children. During our time at the foster home, I benefited by learning about state regulations and administrative rules. I followed the guidelines to care for the children and complete documentation in order to keep the foster care facility licensed. The community was small but so supportive in providing for the home. We also had several opportunities to make new friends and attend a local growing church where the children were able to attend youth groups.

I didn't realize how stressful being a foster parent would be. Not only were we continuing to raise our children still at home, but we were faced with the daily challenges of supporting children who had come from broken homes of addiction, neglect, and abuse.

After two and a half years as full-time house parents, my two youngest children came to me and said, "Mom, you are not our mom. You are stressed out all the time and not being yourself. Whenever we need you, the foster kids need you more."

That was a wake-up call for me. I began to look at myself and realized that I was impatient and unable to successfully remain as a houseparent in the foster home. I turned in my resignation and, shortly thereafter, my husband and I each took separate jobs in the community. With only two of our children left at home, we established a much smaller home for our now family of four.

I became a pharmacy technician where I was again in the medical field. I enjoyed the interaction with the customers, healthcare providers, and nurses not realizing the benefits of learning about pharmacology in years to come.

After two and a half years, our youngest daughter was now a senior in high school. Soon to be empty-nesters, we bought a new home. We were now grandparents and felt content. Life was good. *Then it happened...*

One Sunday morning I was at church listening to the sermon. The pastor was preaching on Joshua and Caleb going into the Promised Land as spies for Israel. The pastor asked the congregation, "What is the promised land in your life that God has given you that you have not possessed?"

Immediately, it was as if God Himself reached down and tapped me on the shoulder and said, "Nursing."

I hadn't even been thinking about going back to school over the last eight years. I really liked my job as a certified pharmacy technician. I liked the people I worked with. But I had a decision to make. *Was I going to possess the Promised Land that God was placing before me? Or was I going to stay in my comfort zone?*

Like most people, I tried negotiating with God. I told Him, "I'll go back to school if my 'old' credits transfer and if I can get the finances to go back to school." I went to work and looked at community colleges where I could complete my prerequisites. I requested my transcript and submitted my application. Much to my surprise (although nothing surprises God), my credits transferred and my application was accepted with funding. The next semester, I once again started classes, this time online, to complete the prerequisites needed to enable me to apply for nursing school.

Of course, the challenge of going back to school, now in my forties and working full time was no easy task. One of the first classes I had to take was, you guessed it, another level of algebra. My faith was once again stretched for me to believe that I could succeed in college and take possession of the promised land to become a nurse. My family was proud of me for being willing to go back to college, but my mother didn't understand why I would do such a thing at my age. For the first time in my life, I had the courage to set aside what others thought and their discouraging comments, even if it was my mom, and moved forward with what I knew God had placed on my heart.

After two semesters of school, it was obvious that I would need to move closer to college to continue classes that were only offered on campus. After our youngest daughter graduated from high school, we sold our house, and my husband and I moved into our 24-foot camper trailer for the next six months. I transferred within the pharmacy to another store, allowing me to continue working full time while I finally completed my prerequisites. The bonus was that we now lived much closer to our oldest daughter's family with our three granddaughters. I received a liberal arts associate's degree when I completed the prerequisites and began applying to nursing schools.

One afternoon my husband mentioned that he noticed a college sign posted that they were receiving applications for the next term of their nursing program. I went to the college to check out the program and it was for a two-year associate's RN degree. I immediately applied, qualified for the funding, took the entrance exam, and was accepted. My promised land was coming clearer into focus. We decided to move closer to the college so we gave the camper to a son for his hunting adventures and moved into a one-bedroom apartment within a few blocks of the campus.

During this time, I realized that I was unhappy with the extra sixty pounds of weight I had gained while cooking three meals a day plus snacks as a foster mom. I had come to realize over the last several years that it's common for staff to gain weight. As caregivers, we often focus on the needs of those we support and take our eyes off of caring for ourselves. We begin to live on caffeine, soda pop, fast food, and processed foods. We volunteer to take on extra shifts and become sleep deprived. We are dehydrated because we don't take the time to drink water throughout our shifts. Alas, as caregivers, our health declines and we get to the point where we are unable to continue to work as a caregiver.

All I knew was that I didn't want to be a 'fat' nurse. I believed that if I was overweight as a nurse, I wouldn't be respected as someone who believed in good health and making good choices because obviously I wasn't doing that for myself.

Divine timing would have it that my pastor (who had preached on the promised land when I believed the Lord was leading me to go back to college to become a nurse) had a daughter - Cristy 'Code Red' Nickel - who is an amazing nutritionist and strength trainer.

I had previously completed one of Cristy's *Code Red Boot Camps* so I knew I could turn to Cristy to help me meet my weight loss goals. I had lost the first 45 lbs on my own, but then I hired Cristy to help me lose the other 15 lbs. and gained my health and strength back. I was feeling great and was so excited to graduate from nursing school at goal weight.

Since that time, Cristy has written a book, <u>The Code Red Revolution: How Thousands of People are Losing Weight and Keeping it Off WITHOUT Pills, Shakes, Diet Foods, or Exercise</u>. She also developed the *30 Day Code Red 10 Pound Takedown* which is an affordable opportunity for you to get back on the path of caring for yourself so you can care for others.

In 2018, I joined my first *10 Pound Takedown* because I had allowed some of my weight to creep back up. The challenge was just what I needed to get me back on the right path of real food, water, sleep, and accountability. Partnering with Cristy has given me a new point of view to believe in myself: *To realize that I can be strong and healthy with a desire to live long and be all God's created me to be as an RN.*

Do you find yourself feeling fatigued, overweight, sleep-deprived, and dehydrated? Do you have difficulty performing your job as a caregiver or caring for your family? I recommend you join your first Code Red 10 Pound Takedown. Go to https://coderedlifestyle.com to access the Cristy "Code Red" Lifestyle.

Lessons Learned:

- **Making a decision based on someone else's agenda can deter us from our own heart's desires.**
- **Making decisions to facilitate someone else's happiness does not mean that you can resolve the condition of their heart.**
- **Making the decision to take care of yourself will increase your courage and confidence.**

Chapter Eight

THE LEARNING CURVE

"The character of the nurse is as important as the knowledge she possesses."
~ Carolyn Javis

Upon being hired as a DD Nurse, I attended orientation. I was confused by all the acronyms: ISP, OAR, DSP, TL, POLST, and so on. I knew a lot of acronyms from the medical field, but this was a whole new language! I spent the next several days learning about the field of supporting individuals with intellectual and developmental disabilities.

Even though I had relationships with many individuals with intellectual and developmental disabilities, I was reminded that all people, with or without disabilities, have the same inherent value and fundamental human rights. My eyes were opened to the isolation individuals experienced because physicians believed that anyone with a disability was better off institutionalized.

I was crushed as I watched the movie, "Where's Molly?" It's a documentary by Jeff Daly about his sister, Molly. When he was six years old, Molly (a toddler at the time) was all of a sudden gone. She just wasn't there anymore. He demanded of his parents, "Where did she go?"

But no one would tell him. The film goes on to share Jeff's journey as years later he begins his search for his sister. I'm teary-eyed every time

Sharlene Meakins, BSN, RN

I've watched it as I've realized the pain families go through when their children are institutionalized, or "warehoused," as Jeff's mother stated in the documentary. This and many more films can be found at https://sproutflix.org. Sproutflix, Making the Invisible Visible. A few years later, a local theater held a Sprout Flix Festival where I had the opportunity to watch several more of their documentaries. The documentary that changed my perspective was when an interviewer asked many individuals with I/DD, "If they could change anything about themselves what would they change?" Their responses were unforgettable! Many said, I wouldn't change anything, I am perfect just the way I am. It was obvious they didn't live with the many lies I had believed about myself because of what I perceived as failures.

I was sobered by what I was learning and realized how sheltered I had been growing up. I remember children born with a developmental disability; both those who had grown up at home and those who had grown up in a facility. But I didn't understand what 'facility' meant. I remember when I was a young girl hearing my doctor's nurse mention that her daughter lived in another place. Later I was able to meet the nurse's daughter at church while she was visiting her family. Born with epilepsy, she also required a wheelchair to transport. Looking back, I realize now that a physician most likely recommended that this beloved daughter be left to grow up in an institution. I believe this broke the nurse's heart because it was obvious to me how much she loved and missed her daughter.

As the newly hired RN for the agency who serves adults with I/DD, I was directed to an office with boxes and files of paperwork that previous nurses had left behind. There was an instruction notebook for community nurses in the I/DD field and administrative rules to learn that applied to 24-hour residential group homes. I began reading through files of persons that had chronic health needs that required a nurse/patient relationship and reviewed their previous assessments and individual care plans. In addition, I reviewed the necessary training and delegations required to be completed for the direct support professionals (DSP). The list of job responsibilities appeared to be endless. I was excited to begin my journey as a DD Nurse, but I had no idea how challenging the learning curve would be; going from what I knew to shooting straight up to what I needed to learn.

Adding to the overwhelming road ahead of me, I was also not met with open arms by several program team leaders and administrators. I went to the executive director and said, "What is the deal? No one seems excited to get to know me. Some of them are actually avoiding me!"

Apparently, a previous DD Nurse had disrespected and belittled the staff with unkind words that implied stupidity and ignorance. My heart was grieved that the staff had been treated so poorly by someone else in my profession and, therefore, they did not look forward to establishing a relationship with the 'new' nurse.

I had never been faced with such difficult and challenging circumstances. It has always been easy for me to build relationships. In this situation, however, it would take being open and asking good questions to remove the walls of resistance previously built within the agency. My first task would be to focus on getting to know the team leaders and administrators in an effort to understand what they had been through and discover how I could gain their confidence and trust. I spent time with each one to better understand their perspective and begin to build relationships with them.

After several weeks, the staff began to open up and I heard amazing stories and learned valuable lessons. I soon recognized their passion for the DD individuals they had been serving for many years.

Over the last several years, I had been on my own journey of learning to stop worrying about what others thought of me. By looking at people in the eyes, I was starting to see their stories and what they had been through. Learning to consider others first and recognizing their needs and desires had helped remove the barriers in communication and relationships. I was able to stop the battle of jealousy and comparison to others by making a choice to rejoice with them in their good fortune, whether it was in relationships, clothing, finances, or their belongings. I learned to be patient and allow the Lord to produce greater kindness and patience within me as I moved forward to build positive relationships with my colleagues.

This journey would begin to take me through the next steps of learning and growing in my career as a nurse. I had only been a licensed RN for a few months and I had so much to learn. I knew that many of the staff had been working in the I/DD community for several years and it was going to be through them that I would learn to be an excellent DD Nurse.

I began working hard and studying the administrative rules for a residential group home while completing the nursing tasks of an RN, doing assessments, writing individual care plans, completing delegations, writing protocols, and learning a new software program. I was so grateful for all the years of administrative and computer technician work that I had done and enjoyed to prepare me for my latest challenge.

This job was turning out to be a good balance of case management nursing, training direct support professionals, and working with individuals with I/DD. The Lord had placed me in the perfect place. However, as the only nurse employed by the agency, being new in the community, and not knowing any other nurses in the field of DD, I was facing this new experience alone.

At first, I didn't *feel* that this was a 'real' nursing career and it was initially difficult to view my new position as that of a nurse. I viewed nursing as traditional nursing tasks - starting an IV, giving injections, drawing blood, etc - like I had been performing during my clinicals. Was I really a nurse? I had to begin to settle this in my own heart. I began to ponder, *What was a nurse? What makes me a nurse? Is it a task or is it heart?*

I was problem-solving and analyzing the health status of individuals with I/DD. I was supporting staff who were direct support professionals who cared for the individuals by providing training and instruction on how to provide safe and proper care. But even more than that, I had a heart of compassion, understanding, and kindness for those individuals with I/DD. I started to recognize my value as a nurse in a non-traditional environment.

I realized I needed to step outside my comfort zone in order to connect with those who have answers to my questions. I started building relationships and making telephone calls to individuals at the state and county offices of the department of human services for DD to ask questions in order to learn how to do my job. I wanted to ensure that I was doing documentation correctly and that I understood the administrative rules for nursing in a 24-hour residential setting.

As I established some footing, I still wanted the opportunity to connect with other DD Nurses in the community so I could have a mentor who had years of experience in order to ask questions and help me along the way. I don't recall how the connection happened, but I met an RN who had been a community DD Nurse for 20 plus years and we began meeting for coffee at least once a month. She also invited another DD Nurse to join us.

I cannot put into words how grateful I was, not only to build relationships with other nurses, but with nurses who were very supportive, willing to answer any questions, and who would give me sound advice. Here were two nurses who understood the unique and complex needs of individuals with I/DD that we served. They understood the state administrative rules and they themselves had been through the licensing process to ensure individuals had stable homes and proper care for many years.

The learning curve continued to go straight up. I grew in knowledge, but my confidence was not growing as quickly as I would have liked. It was then that I was introduced to the Developmental Disabilities Nurses Association (DDNA) https://ddna.org. The mission of DDNA " serves to educate, empower, and advocate for nurses practicing in the specialty of developmental disability nursing." DDNA also helps support DD nursing by communicating and collaborating with local DD nurse networks and groups, helping nurses find support in their own communities. DDNA hosts an annual education conference, providing over 25 hours of exceptional continuing education specific to DD nursing. Attending the conference offers nurses the unique experience of connecting with other DD nurses from across the country and around the globe.

My employer shared with me that previous nurses had attended the DDNA conferences and gained support and training from being involved in the association. I was so grateful that they were willing to invest in me and send me for a greater connection with other DD Nurses and training.

When I arrived at my first DDNA conference, I was astonished that there were so many nurses in the USA and abroad that worked in the I/DD Community. The relationships I began to build would become DDNA relationships for life. The men and women I met had amazing life experiences to share through their hearts of compassion for individuals with I/DD.

Once again, I realized that I was where I belonged, but was sobered by the fact that so many DD Nurses felt as I did, isolated from the 'nursing world.' We were all faced with the challenge of trying to establish excellent care without the day to day support of rubbing shoulders with other nurses. Many of the nurses I met worked for small agencies, like myself, where they were the only nurses. Others were contract nurses for more than one agency where they provided oversight and delegation for several individuals with I/DD that had chronic health diagnoses.

How could I help to close the gap that so many DD Nurses felt in my local community? I began to try to bring nurses together in the field but soon understood that each one of us was so busy that it was difficult to add another meeting or responsibility to our plate on a regular basis. But in the back of my mind, I still wanted to see DD Nurses come together in our local community.

I have come to admire the DDNA Executive Director, Diane Moore,

BSN, RN, CDDN, and those who have and are serving on the DDNA board. One of those individuals is Kathy Brown, RN, BA, CDDN who encouraged me to move forward in my career as a DD Nurse. She introduced me to a vendor, StationMD, www.stationmd.com, at a DDNA conference that focuses on delivering superior care to the most vulnerable populations while also reducing unnecessary hospital use through telemedicine. There I met Dr. Kaufman who shared with me the value of SecureVideo which is a HIPAA compliant video-conferencing application. He went on to state that utilizing the video conferencing was user friendly and would be an excellent tool in starting my own DD Nurse consulting business. This has proven to serve as an excellent tool since I started using it to connect with my clients, complete training which enables me to get eyes on a concern from a distance.

CATHY'S STORY

I find DD Nurses to be more personal and involved with their patients than nurses that work in different environments, like a medical office or hospital. The work really demands a more intimate and involved relationship. DD Nurses are involved with the daily care and routines of the individuals they serve. Developing deep caring relationships is an integral part of work.

A DD Nurse spends many hours researching the intricacies of serving and supporting an individual with I/DD. All of the nurses I have worked with have had to learn the ins and outs of writing protocols for the support needs of the clients that they had a nurse/patient relationship with while following all the State and County requirements. They also attend additional training to continue learning about the latest developments both in nursing in general and DD nursing in particular.

I had the pleasure of attending the DDNA (Developmental Disabilities Nursing Association) conference one year and learned so much more about being a specialized DD Nurse. One of the things I found special about this conference was the tagline, "I'm a DD Nurse, I work everywhere." This message drives home the point that most nurses work in the same location every day, usually a medical office or a hospital, but a DD Nurse works wherever they are needed.

Shar has connected with other DD Nurses in the area to have a network of like-minded peers to discuss thoughts, protocols, concerns, and also share triumphs. I believe this networking to be the most useful tool in a DD Nurse's toolbox.

Lessons Learned:

- **All people, with or without disabilities, have the same inherent value and fundamental human rights.**
- **It is essential that DD Nurses serve as an understanding compassionate team player to ensure that individuals with I/DD be provided holistic care.**
- **An individual's care team provides the DD Nurse information that is invaluable in order to provide accurate support documents.**
- **The DDNA is an essential source of training and support for every DDNA to grow in her knowledge, training, and certification.**

Chapter Nine

COMMUNICATION AND BUILDING TRUST

"They may forget your name, but they will never forget how you made them feel."
~ Maya Angelou

As the months turned into years, I frequently heard comments such as, "Shar, you're a really good nurse."

My executive director was quick to point out that people not only liked me, *they trusted me*. Merriam-Webster defines trust as, "assured reliance on the character, ability, strength, or truth of someone or something." That spoke volumes to me. My desire was for the staff to trust me. I wanted them to feel that they were able to rely on me. I wanted them to feel free to ask questions without fear of ridicule. And I wanted them to receive my instruction to keep the individuals in our care healthy and safe.

Looking back, I realized that I had developed a lifestyle of giving honor and respect to individuals with intellectual and developmental disabilities. I had learned to communicate with kindness, patience, and respect. I had gained skills to listen carefully and observe with the intent to understand what they were communicating. The trust I received over the years had been developed through a sincere interest, a smile, and positive body language.

Now I was in a new arena. I needed to build the trust of healthcare and mental health providers. There were incidents when I would support an individual during a clinical visit and it was difficult to gain a provider's trust, as I asked questions or made suggestions for the individual's care. One particular provider accused me of practicing outside my scope of practice. I took this as an indication that I needed to grow in my communication skills. I wanted to ensure I was communicating observations, facts, and asking quality questions in order to develop a clear plan of care.

It's essential that I gain the trust of family members and guardians of an individual with whom I have a nurse/patient relationship. One guardian said to me that I was just another nurse that would come and go and that I wouldn't be with the agency long. That was *six years* ago, but it made me pause and try to look through their eyes. I wanted to try to understand the hurt they had experienced as parents with an only child who would never have the joy of an independent life, nor would they ever experience being grandparents. I began to think about all the disappointments and adjustments a parent in their shoes would experience.

Guardians may think that we don't have their child's best interest in mind when we discuss health concerns and treatments, but we really do. Of course, we will never replace the love and oversight of a parent or family guardian, but we aim to provide support as best we can.

Another area of pain is the ups and downs for individuals when support staff, such as nurses and caregivers, come and go in their lives with so few community friends with stability. Individuals with I/DD typically only have paid staff in their lives and don't experience life long friendships and family relationships as you and I do. Trust is definitely difficult to build without longevity.

Each individual I support comes from unique experiences and backgrounds. Some have been institutionalized because physicians deemed that their families could not care for them. Others have been placed in care because their parents are physically unable to care for them any longer or they have passed away.

One such individual, I'll call Sally, had been placed in 24-hour residential care because her health had been failing. Sally could no longer live independently in her own apartment. Her mother had been a huge part of Sally's life. She had assisted her with medications, meal preparation, and cleaning. But Sally's mom had passed away and she was having a difficult time adjusting to our recommendations for leading a safe and healthy lifestyle.

Norma would often tell me that I wasn't a real nurse because I didn't wear a uniform. But when I would arrive in scrubs, she told me I still wasn't a nurse because I didn't have a name badge. *Oi vey!*

I learned from this experience that not every individual I supported would choose to trust me or follow instructions on how to make good choices for their health and safety. Once I recognized that each individual had their own choices to make and that I didn't need to carry the pressure of their compliance on my shoulders, I was free to serve them without expectation while still doing my best to meet their healthcare needs. I can only implement what I know as best-practice care, whether they are willing to receive it or not.

I found it true that every individual and staff that I would support or train were each very much individuals with their own experiences and that each one would interpret me as a nurse through different eyes.

I had the privilege of supporting Renae, a woman who was close to my age who was a delight to get to know and spend time with while visiting over a cup of coffee. I learned a difficult lesson through her family, however. When Renae had gotten ill and admitted to the hospital, the family turned their anger towards me. They indicated that it was my fault that Renae had been hospitalized because I wasn't providing proper care and instruction. How disturbing to experience the ridicule of someone I had only met a couple of times and that they would imply to the nursing board that I was neglectful!

From this experience, I gained a better understanding of how critically important it was that I protect my license and career as a nurse. I was traumatized by this experience of being falsely accused. It would take me more than a year to shake off the idea that there could be those that would point blame in order to extinguish their own regret. I had to choose not to give up and run the other way. I had to reject the thought: *Wouldn't it be easier just to work at a clinic, clock in 8-5, and go home at night without carrying the responsibility of being on-call?*

Shortly thereafter, my responsibilities at the agency grew. I began training new staff on medical management, medication administration, and I became a First Aid and CPR/AED instructor. I was surprised to find out how much I enjoyed teaching and developing training presentations. I started seeing myself through new eyes and recognizing that my desires and abilities were broader than I imagined. I think we often don't step out of our comfort zones due to our fear of failure.

I decided to complete my Bachelor of Science in Nursing (BSN) degree online. [I also contemplated getting my master's in either education or administration but the outcome didn't outweigh the cost.] The executive director pointed out that acquiring certifications was very valuable and that the Developmental Disabilities Nurse Association (DDNA) offered certification for the DD Nurse (CDDN). I could also acquire certification in other areas that were supportive in the I/DD Community like mental health and memory care which I really enjoyed in clinicals. Since individuals with I/DD are living longer, understanding dementia care was becoming an increased need.

I applied to the DDNA to be considered for the certification exam that was being offered at the next DDNA conference. I was able to sit for the exam, but the director of the association shared with me that the exam was based on years of experience, preferably five years or more, in the field of DD. I was still fairly new not only in the field, but also as a nurse. I went ahead to take the exam at the conference and did not pass. I wasn't discouraged though because I was confident that I was where I belonged as a nurse and that I would continue to grow in my knowledge to become a CDDN. Someone recommended a textbook to me that was helpful as I continued to study for the exam (I still had time within my application time frame to test again).

Each day has brought new awareness and experiences that have helped me understand the career of being a DD Nurse. One such experience was the day I received an urgent telephone call from the director of the agency who needed me to come to a group home's licensing onsite and review immediately. Every two years, each program's license is up for review and a team of State employees comes to the home to perform an 'onsite' to ensure that the individuals residing there are doing well, that we are addressing their medical needs appropriately, that the home is safe, and we are keeping proper documentation for monitoring the individual's overall needs and desires.

I had only observed one onsite from a distance (at a home where I did not support an individual) so I had not been accustomed to attending these reviews. However, there were some concerns at this particular program. I knew walking in that I would need to build a positive rapport and be teachable in order to understand any administrative rule I was not following properly and make any necessary corrections. I quickly realized though that the program director had not done a good job of informing me of medical needs and keeping me abreast of concerns with the individuals who had nurse/patient relationships with me.

I then became aware that I assumed the staff would keep me in the loop regarding the status of any individual I was providing nursing oversight for. *Assuming* would become a new red flag for me. I could not *assume* the staff understood my support documents or vocabulary. I could not *assume* that they understood a health concern since they themselves may have never seen or experienced it.

I gladly worked with the onsite reviewer and was able to make the necessary corrections I needed to address. I also made the necessary contacts with the healthcare provider to clarify orders. I was so grateful for this experience and, from there on out, I was informed when onsites were being done where an individual I had a nurse/patient relationship was involved. Thereafter, I was so grateful when the onsite reviewer notified the executive director to inform him of nursing board training I could receive specifically designated for community and DD nursing. I was more than willing to attend classes, webinars, and complete online instruction. As a result, I continued to grow more in my understanding of the responsibility of being a community DD Nurse.

Now I had a new perspective that I could communicate with staff about the importance of monitoring and documentation which also included ensuring that I was notified with concerns. I had become more aware of the need to be thorough in writing protocols, care plans, and instructions for the staff to follow so they were not in 'medical jargon' but written in layman terms, easy to read and understand.

I learned that in writing an individual's care plan, not only do you need to indicate the expected outcome, but identify what the interventions are, who is responsible for the interventions, and the location of the care plan.

For example:

Plan/Goal	Implementation/Intervention	Evaluation
To prevent events of aspiration of coughing or choking while eating.	Staff are to prepare food and fluids as outlined in the speech/language therapist guidelines and the Aspiration Protocol is located in _____.	Completed during nursing reviews or updated as needed with events of aspiration or change in health status.

Reminder: Again, these care plans are not written for nurses. It is essential that the language is easy for staff to understand and follow in the individual's care. All staff must be trained on the care plans with a documented training log record.

The policies, procedures, and administrative rules can be a challenge to manage. After three years of experience with the agency, I said to the director, "Will I ever learn this job?"

He responded, "No, the administrative rules and oversight is ever-changing with the State and the Federal government so it's always evolving."

As a DD Nurse, we must first and foremost understand the scope of practice and the board of nursing rules. I again chose not to lose heart, but continue to be positive and confident that I would do my best to be an excellent DD Nurse.

After several months, it was time to again take the CDDN exam within the allotted time I had before the approved application would expire. I was "feeling" more confident since I had studied the textbook thoroughly and had taken the practice tests online. However, this would be a proctored test at a testing site, and once again it was timed which has always placed pressure on me to read and process much more quickly than I preferred.

As you recall, by no means did I see myself as an excellent student but I would apply myself. In fact, during college, an instructor and I visited when I was distraught over the challenges of the class. The instructor explained to me that once I graduated as a nurse, a patient would not ask what grades I got in class; they would assess and respond to my care and compassion. The instructor also went on to say that if she had to choose between a young nurse who got straight A's or myself, a compassionate nurse with years of life experience and common sense, she would choose me.

After completing the CDDN exam at the testing site, I felt pretty good, but it was not a test that you could know the results of once you were done. I had to wait for the results over the next several weeks. The day I received the letter that I had not passed, I was disappointed. I had to stop and recognize that my value as a DD Nurse wasn't in a certification. I knew I was a good DD Nurse but that I definitely had more room and years to grow in my ability to acquire a certification. I would not give up!

Brian's Story

When Shar and I met years ago for an interview, she had recently acquired nursing licensure and was excited, energized, and completely empathetic. It wasn't very long into the interview when I could see the life experience, knowledge, wisdom, and values she was bringing to the table. Much of her previous work experience was also quite applicable.

Our agency was a residential provider for persons with I/DD and co-occurring medical, mental health diagnoses. We had lost our beloved head of nursing, Jane Duke, RN, to cancer in recent years. We had hired some very proficient interim nurses but needed someone else in the role that was more representative of our mission, vision, and values to lead our medical and nursing support employing their profession with both heart and mind. Jane had left a big hole and big shoes to fill. And, the interim nurses had not been able to build the level of trust or relationship with our stakeholders to the degree we preferred. In short, Jane's shoes were too big for these very qualified and experienced professionals.

The nurse we hired was going to have to work very hard to earn trust and respect. Shar's limitless empathy and understanding provided her the in-road she needed. She is professional, approachable, fair, respectful, and kind. Providing absolute adherence to nursing standards and ethics is essential.

I have a standard I share within our organization. It comes from having a family member with I/DD, Autism, Challenging Behavior, Seizures, and significant Allergies. My standard is, "If what we are doing isn't good enough for you, your family or friends, then it isn't good enough for those we are supporting." In short, without any hesitation or reserve, I would be honored to have Shar as my family's nurse. I have the highest regard for her as a professional and as a fellow human.

As I move to the close of my career (retirement is two years away), I find myself looking back, and I've come to understand that finding love in what we do is our ultimate gift to ourselves and others. The people I've met, supported, and worked alongside in this helping field have impacted the entirety of who I've become and how I will see the contributions I've made.

Lessons Learned:

- **An essential component as a DD Nurse is building trust in your relationships with each person involved in the DD Community.**
- **Each day brings new awareness from experiences that help provide understanding in the career of supporting the I/DD Community.**
- **As a DD Nurse, we must first and foremost understand the scope of practice, the board of nursing rules, and the State administrative rules for the Department of Human Services for DD.**

Chapter Ten

RECOGNIZING VALUE

*"You could be the next person to succeed
if you choose to learn from successful people instead of being envious of them.
Moreover, aren't they successful because they learned
and continue to learn from others?"
- Edmond Mbiaka*

After observing Cristy "Code Red" Nickel's success, I proclaimed to myself and others, "I'm going to have my own business someday!"

I wanted to hire a business coach and surround myself with mentors who knew me and who understood my desire to invest in the I/DD Community. I started to reach out with my questions: *How do I start a business? How do I surround myself with others who have been consultants and where do I begin?* Surprisingly, the answers came fairly quickly through my acquaintances and mentors who had started their own businesses. I was encouraged to know that I could follow my heart and walk in my desires.

I was amazed to discover how supportive my family and friends were. I was surrounded by support, wise counsel, encouragement, and prayer. Interestingly, around the same time, I was at a meeting where we discussed the shortage of nurses in the I/DD Community and a gentleman turned to me and said that I needed to be cloned. I laughed, but later I started to ponder, *How could I be cloned? Why am I worth cloning? What do I know about DD nursing that other nurses would want to know? What questions did I have as a DD Nurse that I could answer for someone else? How does a nurse make a difference in the I/DD Community?*

Throughout my life's journey, I have always had a desire to do more. I've often thought that I was discontent, but in reality, I was simply looking for the next opportunity that would expand my horizons. I have enjoyed every job that I have ever had. It didn't matter if it was waiting tables, cleaning toilets, being a receptionist, an administrative assistant, computer technician, pharmacy technician, caregiver, etc. I have approached each job as a chance to look for better ways to do the job and sought to create new tools for the next employee. God created me to be innovative, with a desire to make a difference by reaching out, encouraging, and investing in others - even if it's simply through a smile.

What about you? Have you hit roadblocks in your life?

Are you in 'drive' but not experiencing any forward momentum?

Cristy wanted to move forward in her personal and professional goals, but she was stuck in a cycle of working hard yet merely surviving on a poverty income. All that was about to change when a woman named Natasha Hazlett hired her as a weight-loss coach. When Cristy realized who Natasha was and her popularity as a branding coach, she hired Natasha to help her turn her business around. Over the next two years, Cristy was able to completely transform her business into a multi-million dollar company that has changed not only her life but the thousands of people who have joined the 'Code Red' movement.

When I witnessed Cristy's business take off, I, too, wanted to experience the life-changing benefits of living a life of Unstoppable Influence. I purchased Natasha's book, **Unstoppable Influence: Be You, Be Fearless, Transform Lives**, and devoured it. Next, I joined one of Natasha's 21-Day Challenges and began to see my life transform. I was able to identify and release toxic thinking and limiting beliefs that I'd held for years. As a result, I developed the courage to put my dreams on paper and hit the gas on my own personal journey of Unstoppable Influence.

You can also learn how to drive around the roadblocks to your dreams and experience a life of miracles as an Unstoppable Influencer. To discover more, go to: https://unstoppable.idevaffiliate.com/239.html.

When I started the position as a DD Nurse, others in the community couldn't understand what I did as a nurse. I didn't fit into the typical picture of what people envisioned as a nursing career. At the 25th Annual DDNA Conference, one of the founding members handed out a pinback button that read: *I am a DD Nurse and I work everywhere.*

It was true! My position as a DD Nurse was far from mundane. My weeks are filled with opportunities to serve by being a part of an individual's support team, attending healthcare and/or mental health appointments which may include an emergency department visit, completing online reviews of their health tracking, faxing or calling providers and/or the pharmacy for necessary orders and asking questions about their care. This position serves as more of an overall care management position with the benefit of building wonderful relationships with individuals with I/DD, their staff, guardians, family members, case managers, healthcare providers, occupational and speech-language therapists, physical therapists, and mental health providers. The list goes on and on. You rely on so many people who serve in the I/DD community to meet every need of the individual being supported.

My value is in what I have to offer other nurses and direct support professionals (DSP) from my experience with building positive, influential relationships in the I/DD community and implementing the necessary administrative rules that have been put in place to ensure that each person with I/DD can experience a fulfilled life of choice.

Sharlene Meakins, BSN, RN

Wynter's Story

I met Shar during a time when I provided Case Management services to the I/DD population. Shar was new to providing direct nursing services for a 24-hour provider agency serving those with I/DD. Her compassion for her clients, personal integrity, and sense of responsibility to those whom she provided her services was astonishing.

Working with Shar came effortlessly. She was intrigued to learn "our" way of producing protocols, such as fatal four, licensing expectations and when implementing a nursing care plan. The State requires complex documentation, outside of the lengthy documentation already required by an RN in order to support the individuals with I/DD.

I had worked with many nurses prior to Shar. Many of the nurses were not employed by an agency or group home for individuals with I/DD. But they were contracted through the State to provide direct care nursing services. When working in a capacity with such a fragile population, it is always valuable to find a nurse with a great deal of empathy. I have experienced working with nurses who struggled to assimilate the idea of care for the I/DD community. I realized that this nurse didn't just treat her encounters as a "job" as most do. Shar wanted to make a difference. She was determined to help others and it showed.

As we grow through life experiences, both good and bad, we take some truth from each of these events. Showing perseverance in each situation plays such an influential role on a team. A DD Nurse's experience provides new perspectives and considerable knowledge, which brings with it respect and value. My desire is to see more nurses, like Shar, who exemplify this quality of care provided to those with I/DD.

Lessons Learned:

- Celebrate and rejoice over other people's successes; realize you can experience your own success as a result of your heart to make a difference.
- Recognize the value of those in authority; they have a lot to offer and will help you grow in your understanding.
- Many people work together to meet the needs of the individual being supported; you must learn to rely on each other.

Chapter Eleven

THE VALUE OF IMPLEMENTING PROFESSIONAL INSIGHT

"Alone we can do so little; together we can do so much."
— Helen Keller

I have also come to recognize the value of other professionals that provide various services to support individuals. Such an individual is Audra, the mother I met when my daughter was working as a personal support worker for her child. I provided delegation training for her daughter's personal support workers and grew to admire her passion for providing holistic care for her daughter.

AUDRA'S STORY

I am a second career Nutritionist focusing on medical nutrition therapy, herbal medicine, and holistic healing. I gratefully support any person seeking optimal health but have a special calling for those with complex medical and special needs. I met Nurse Shar before my career changed to nutrition. Meeting up with Shar was all part of an unexpected and meaningful journey!

I found this path via my own special needs child. To be frank, my daughter was dying. *Starving* to be specific. And, in a poignant moment in my life while she gagged and retched on her "medical formula," I wondered why she couldn't have "real" food? Everything changed at that moment and we began our journey to true wellness. I read everything I could get my hands on in terms of food as medicine and herbal supports.

Through that journey, I weaned my very complex daughter from every pharmaceutical medication and successfully replaced them with food and herbs. She gained weight and began to smile, laugh, play, and thrive!

We were blessed to have nurse Shar come on board to collaborate with our team, and even through tough times, with her support we were able to enjoy the highest quality of life possible!

Once I realized I needed to share this gift with the world, I earned my master's degree at The National University of Natural Medicine and, with the mentorship of Shar, engaged in an internship in a group home setting that supports adults with developmental disabilities. During my time at the group home, I was able to share nourishing and delicious food with the clients and staff. We witnessed incredible results in a short period of time. One example is with a client who was able to release excess weight and begin ambulating, increasing circulation to her extremities and allowing her to engage in more social activity. This internship went so well, that I am honored to report I now contract with this organization.

I wholeheartedly believe in a holistic approach and a large portion of that concept is building a collaborative team to support the individual. I believe all humans have the right to access healthy, delicious food and compassionate, integrated healthcare with equity. If you would like to invite me to your team or learn more about me, please visit my webpage www.loveaudra.com.

Lessons Learned:

- Recognize the value of those who provide services that will facilitate holistic support for individuals to have a lifestyle of health and wellness.
- By providing information and opportunities for individuals to make life-style changes helps implement positive outcomes.
- Blessings come in the form of relationships that uphold one another.

Chapter Twelve

MENTORING TO MAKE A DIFFERENCE

*"There is no greater disability in society
than the inability to see a person as more."
~ Robert M. Hensel*

As evident throughout this book, I have crossed paths with many people who have made a significant difference in my life. I am confident you also can name a list of people who have taken the time to impart wisdom, skills, and understanding to you during your lifetime. I can think of many times that I would have given up on what I was doing, whether it be college, work, or even walk and grow in my faith if I didn't have people in my life who believed in me.

As a result, I find myself often telling others to pursue their dreams and not give up. I purposely communicate with others the importance of learning and growing despite their perceived weaknesses, lies they believe about themselves, and their circumstances.

As a DD Nurse, we often are not given the tools we need without the mentoring of another DD Nurse. Not only are we following our scope of practice through the Board of Nursing, but we are following the administrative rules within a State's Department of Human Services. The nurse is a key player in assessing an individual's health risks and the annual needs assessment for those with chronic health conditions. Often, the DD Nurse is partnering with the provider of the individual's behavioral needs assessment to provide an understanding of mental health and physical health. These are documented for the individual's support plan.

Some individuals are able to communicate their needs and desires while others may be nonverbal and unable to understand their needs. Or an individual may be capable of making a simple decision such as agreeing to an exam but unable to make an informed decision on the need for a procedure. Thus, it's important to acknowledge the value of an individual support plan team that includes a DD Nurse who can serve as an advocate for the individual.

The difficulty often arises when an individual with developmental disabilities makes bad personal choices as many of us do. For example, an individual who has been diagnosed with sleep apnea and congestive heart failure has been advised by their physician to stop smoking. However, the individual declares to his physician that they will not quit smoking, thus placing the individual's support team in a difficult situation. We try to support them and encourage them to make good health choices.

Also, individuals, guardians, health care representatives, and their support team are being compelled to make decisions that involve advance directives when they are hospitalized. This can be very challenging when many don't recognize the value of life, which is not dependent on our level of functionality.

Do you find yourself relating to my experience or do you desire to pursue your own Path of Purpose? You will never regret following your heart no matter how many turns, ruts and climbs you take. There is nothing better than recognizing that your Creator has a plan for your life and as you take a hold of that truth, you too can become all you were meant to be.

Lessons Learned:

- **Intentionally communicate with others the importance of learning and growing despite their perceived weaknesses, lies they believe about themselves, and their circumstances.**
- **Coming alongside others to encourage, support, and help them be successful brings new opportunities to make a difference.**
- **Recognize your personal value by seeing that your Creator has an amazing plan for your life.**

Chapter Thirteen

FACING THE UNEXPECTED

*"We could never learn to be brave and patient
if there were only joy in the world."
- Helen Keller*

When you begin any new career, you soon find out that your formal education only scratched the surface of what you have ahead of you. I quickly learned that I needed to listen to those who had known the individuals we were serving for several years. This allowed me to see the bigger picture and begin to put the pieces of the puzzle together on how I could best support each individual's healthcare needs.

I learned that communication among the team leader, direct support professionals, and myself was crucial. I realized that they were attacking my knowledge as a nurse but that together we could problem-solve based on medical history and current signs and symptoms. True teamwork began when the staff recognized that I wanted to learn from them.

The years of experience that were represented in the office alone was amazing. When I was initially interviewed for the DD Nurse position, I asked both of the people interviewing me how many years of experience they have in the DD field and how long had they both been with the agency? One of them had been there for 18 years with several years of experience before that and the other one had been with the agency for twenty years. I was sold! If this career drew people in with years of loyalty, I could take my chances.

I soon understood that I needed to discuss with an individual their needs and desires which included others in their circle of influence. This was true when it came to working with the primary care physician, pharmacists, behavior specialists, counselors, physical therapists, occupational therapists, numerous physician specialists, and the list goes on. But first and foremost is the importance of building a relationship with an individual's family and guardian whenever possible.

The value of building these relationships gives us as DD Nurses a greater capacity to provide the necessary support and advocacy for those with whom we have a professional healthcare connection.

I truly enjoy building relationships with those that provide support in the I/DD Community as well as the delightful relationships I have built with amazing individuals that have overcome more obstacles than most in just maneuvering everyday life. I'm privileged that my position as a DD Nurse is significant and purposeful in making a difference in other's lives.

Over the years, I have met several parents and families who have amazing resilience to overcome obstacles and learn how to make adjustments in life in order to care for one another. This requires many medical interventions and an enormous learning curve. I smile when I see the family, especially children, learn how to be supportive and perform duties to care for a sibling with intellectual or developmental disabilities.

I met one such family last year and have followed them on social media. They are willing to share the ups and downs of caring for a son with cerebral palsy who is bound to a wheelchair, breathes through a tracheostomy, and eats through a gastric-tube. All of this brings with it the challenge of finding enough nursing support and respite. Let's hear from Shanon who, like many moms with a child with a disability, make a difference in the lives of their family, friends, and neighbors. Their love and support extend far beyond their own corner of the world.

Shanon's Story

Why can't you take care of your own child?

I needed help, but I was too scared to ask. I felt *less than*... not being able to be all the things I was called to be. There were so many days of tears and struggle just to be able to keep him alive. Not to mention all the duties I have as a wife and a mother of two. The moment I'd be gone to take time for anyone other than Justin's "special needs" it seems like we would end up in the hospital. I was stretched super thin.

Asking for help was the only way out. Not just help physically, I also needed help with the mental and spiritual battle of caring for a son with special needs.

The first time I received assistance was a few hours a week in respite care. I cherished that time because it meant I could devote two full hours to Justin's sister. So as a mother I'm multitasking and went grocery shopping with just her. It still brings tears to my eyes knowing our time at the store was the only chance I had to fully devote to her during that season of our lives.

When full nursing was available, I stopped beating myself up for needing help. I opened my heart and my home to the most wonderful ladies who brought a quality of care to my son that allowed me to bring a quality of care to not only my other children but to my husband and to myself.

Twenty years later, I look back on the blessings that each nurse has played in our life. And Justin in theirs. Having the help didn't just keep him alive and thriving, but the whole family.

I am truly blessed and grateful that I put down my ego and opened my home for the nurses that have become part of our family. Home health nursing equals living vitality by nurturing. Thank you to all the nurses out there! And my message to other parents of special needs children is, "If you question having a nurse come into your home, don't! The answer is YES!!"

***

I have also come to highly respect a couple who worked at the masters level in the Department of Health Services for DD. This couple themselves have a son with cerebral palsy that is a friend and encouragement to everyone he meets. Even though he is nonverbal, he uses his designated form of sign, a communication board, cards, and expression to communicate. He is very social, enjoys connections with the people he meets at his home, church, and in the community. His parents, by their example, have set a high standard of expectations for life, health, and joy which has served their son very well. It has been a pleasure to serve him and his parents.

NATHAN'S STORY

Our introduction to Shar was through quite an awkward meeting about six years ago. My son's support team wasn't fully acquainted yet. Our son, now 40 years old, was a new client for the agency and Shar's open and warm approach made the whole meeting successful.

Even though he has complicated medical support needs, Shar's approach to Nathan was also warm and accepting as well. She immediately sought to learn how to communicate with Nathan. She worked to spend quality time with him and did not become discouraged with the amount of time it took to learn his signs and sounds. Now Nathan is very comfortable with Shar, both at home and in medical settings. We feel anyone who cares enough to put in the time to get to know, communicate with, and care about our son, is a friend of ours.

Nathan needs protocols to help people know what to do with and for him in a possible emergency. Everything from uncontrolled seizures to heat exhaustion requires detailed planning and preparation. As an "involved" parent getting the details right is extremely important to me. It's hard for people to work so closely with me because I want to go over it and over it and over it…repeatedly. Shar takes my obsessive detail orientation regarding my son in stride. And yes, we've completed all those protocols.

When an unusual event occurs for Nathan, his support staff write an incident report. Often these include medical concerns. Shar is readily available and consults with us, as well as staff, respectfully, and compassionately. Everyone is happy to have Shar come in to consult, including Nathan. Being cooperative and kind, not authoritarian or rigid, shows why she's great at working with us and Nathan's team. Understandably, we have a lot of confidence in Shar.

***

I so enjoy working with individuals when their parents and family are involved in their lives. Sadly, individuals with a developmental disability are isolated from their families. However, that is not the case with Carol and her daughters. A woman with strong Christian values, Carol has worked hard to hold her family together with loyalty and dedication.

Carol's Story

My name is Carol and I am the mother of three developmentally disabled daughters. My oldest daughter was born blind, having no vision in the right eye and very limited in the left, and no speech. She had a stroke just before her first birthday and lost the use of the right side of her body, but was erroneously diagnosed as being epileptic and put on medication. None of the doctors noted the stroke until many years later.

Then at eight and a half months old, one of my twins was moving around the house in her walker and tipped it over hitting her head, causing a neck injury. She also was diagnosed with a seizure disorder and prescribed medication for it. It did sort of control the seizures but she began regressing, losing all the things she had been doing to the point of being a vegetable. In desperation, we went to another doctor who found the neck injury and treated it, but to no avail as her brain had been deprived of oxygen for so long that she had severe brain damage. As a result, more handicapping conditions developed.

My other twin started making unusual sounds during the early hours of the morning and hearing the noises I went into her bedroom to find her seizing. She also was diagnosed as having a seizure variant and put on medication. Her type of seizure affects her memory so she has lost the ability to do many things that she could do previously.

When the girls came of school age, there was no classroom for them. So our next battle was how to get a classroom for our children by the time school would start in the fall. We also succeeded in getting bus service for our children.

After high school, I knew that I would be unable to care for them on my salary and the best option seemed to be placement in local group homes near the family. It was a painful decision to do this, but I learned shortly that it was a good decision. The agency and the caretakers truly cared for them and worked very hard to give them a very good life and life experiences.

It was during this time that I met Shar who was our agency nurse. She impressed me with her deep caring concern for all of her patients, not just my daughters. She was always right there for her patients, night or day, or whatever the circumstances. She communicated and explained things the other professionals told us but may not have explained as thoroughly as we needed. She answered my questions and presented all the options. If there were challenges with some of the doctors or other professionals, she would accompany me to the next appointment to assist in getting them to listen to what I had to say.

I really believe that because of Shar's passion, love, and caring for her patients and their families, that our children are enjoying a much better quality of life. Thank you, Shar!

Lessons Learned:

- **The value of building relationships with an individual's family gives DD Nurses a greater capacity to provide the necessary support and advocacy for those with whom you have a professional healthcare connection.**
- **Be genuine as a person and as a DD Nurse to show your heart and be a true reflection of compassion, kindness, and care.**
- **Understand that each of you is a key player in the team of supporting an individual with I/DD and their family; each person's role on the team is of great value.**

Chapter Fourteen

DIRECT SUPPORT PROFESSIONALS ARE OUR HEROS

"The simple act of caring is heroic."
~ Edward Albert

According to America's Direct Support Workforce Crisis: Report to the President 2017, "The direct support workforce is one of the highest-demand workforces in the U.S. In 2015, there were nearly 4.5 million direct support workers identified in the three categories of personal care assistance, home health aide, and nursing."

As of 2018, 7.3 million individuals with intellectual or developmental disabilities in the United States have an overwhelming lack of direct support professionals (DSP) due to an immense turnover rate.

The lack of DSPs is often primarily due to the low pay scale for a DSP (starting at minimum wage) along with the possibility of supporting an individual with severe medical needs or behavioral outbursts. The lack of DSPs can mean working long exhausting hours that results in burnout. Therefore, it is essential to understand the value of a DSP.

As I shared previously, I had the privilege of working as a DSP for a 24-hour residential group home for individuals with DD while waiting for my state RN license. I had no idea how valuable this experience would prove to be.

Even though my time as a DSP was short, it did not take long as a new DD Nurse for me to realize that I needed the DSP's perspective on the health status of an individual. A DSP works with the DD individuals day in and day out. It is the DSP that assists them in completing their activities of daily living (ADLs). They are the ones that know the individual most intimately - their likes and dislikes, their goals, who their family members are, etc. I depend on them and listen carefully to their observations, concerns, and questions. Not only do the DD individuals need to trust a DD Nurse, but even more so the DSP so they are willing to call and know that the nurse will listen to them and take their observations seriously.

Often within an agency, it becomes the DD Nurse's responsibility to train the medical management procedures and policies. I personally worked with a DSP, a woman with over 18 years of experience, to build a foundation for DSPs to understand their health-related responsibilities. We express the importance of staff using their senses to determine if there is a change in an individual's physical and mental health status. They must take the time to observe an individual's overall physical appearance - the color of their skin, mobility, any signs of pain, monitoring intake and elimination, and mental health status. Do they hear a respiratory change, smell a difference in their elimination, feel a change in their skin temperature or texture, or observe an individual with confusion or increased irritability?

I tell staff that if they sense that something is wrong or different to "listen to their gut" because they are probably correct. Just because they may be the most recent staff hired, does not mean that they can not determine a change of health status in the individual they are supporting. In fact, the opposite may be true. Often, when we are with an individual day in and day out for several months or even years, we become unaware of their slow health changes. Then when a new set of eyes is involved, the staff may notice abnormalities quicker. I do not negate concerns reported to me by a new staff just because they've not known the individual long.

When providing DSPs verbal or written instructions, I recognize that not everyone has had the same life experiences. Therefore, I've learned to ask questions to obtain a better picture of what is taking place and not assume that my communication is clear. I find that I may be quick to blame a staff member for a mistake that has taken place in an individual's care when really it's been due to a lack of training or understanding.

As humans, when we see an error, we have a tendency to be quick to point the finger at someone when the truth is, the person is not the problem. Often the problem is the problem. *Does the DSP have the written instructions available to complete a specific task correctly? Is the DSP given the tools to complete a task or are they needing to improvise? Is the staff fearful of asking questions?* I myself was not given much instruction in how to care for the individuals with I/DD prior to starting my first shift. I was grateful that I was a nurse and that I had the confidence to problem-solve. I was especially thankful that the individuals I was serving were verbal and could communicate their needs.

The DSPs in the DD field are truly our heroes. They make a difference in the lives of those they provide support for every day. They not only provide support for daily hygiene, dressing, meals, and medications, they also provide transportation for work and activities. I remind staff that they are carrying a big daily load, not only with the daily routines, but with chronic health issues, mobility support, and the acute concerns that arise.

As a result, I remind staff that it is so important for them to care for themselves and intentionally get enough sleep, exercise, consume a balanced diet, and stay hydrated. We must each take steps to ensure that we are healthy in order to care for someone else whether that be for our employment, family, or friends. The individuals we support and the team of other staff are depending on us to be there for our shift. My experience is that not only do we depend on one another but the individuals we serve anticipate staff being there for their shift. Often they know the schedule of the staff better than we ourselves. The individuals look forward to the staff coming in for their shift and their time together.

One might recognize that the result of a DSP or any support staff, such as a nurse, working long-term with an individual, may often become emotionally attached. Even though we are serving in a professional capacity, we are human and we develop bonds with those we serve. The downfall of this can be that we have a tendency to "parent" an adult with I/DD. We take on more responsibility than is ours to carry. We begin to make decisions based on what "I" would do, rather than what the individual desires.

It's difficult to provide a balance between providing safety and implementing control. Therefore, it is important for staff to speak up and privately share observations that are made when another staff is 'parenting.' What does parenting look like? I've observed staff using terms of endearment. For instance, they might start calling individuals honey, sweetheart, dear, or buddy. This seemingly harmless practice places the caregiver in an overseeing role rather than a supporting role. It's important that we give dignity to those we support. Not just by providing modesty while providing showers, comfort care, and dressing, we need to also give dignity by using a person's name. We all want to be respected and recognized by our name which gives us the recognition of being a unique person with needs, dreams, goals, and purpose.

A difficult season in a DSP's life is when an individual has been diagnosed with a terminal or chronic illness which reduces their life expectancy. According to recent studies, individuals with I/DD 35 years ago were living shorter lives, but now their life expectancy is equal to that of the average person living in the United States. As support staff, we must know and understand our patient's desires around end-of-life issues and religious needs. Just as it's difficult to say goodbye to a family member or friend, it can be just as difficult to say goodbye to someone you've supported for several months or even years.

Therefore, it's important to acknowledge the grieving process in one another as we see the individual declining. We must recognize that not all staff have experienced losing someone to death. Caregivers often "push through" and don't take the time they need to care for their own emotional and mental health which can lead to burnout. I often remind staff that working in a shift environment, that they don't have to always say "yes" when someone calls in sick or needs to take a day off. Caregivers are "fixers." We have a tendency to want to take care of everyone when we see a need while ignoring our own needs. Working an extra shift, several days in a row without a day off does not pay off in the long run since they become vulnerable to fatigue and illness.

Last but not least, DSPs like all of us, need recognition for our work. Too often we are quick to blame, pointing out errors and shortcomings, but we need to acknowledge all the positive accomplishments they make as well. It's true, DSPs do not get paid their worth, despite the fact they are caring for another human being. Therefore, our words and gifts of appreciation, affirmation, and thanks go a long way. Anytime we make the effort to acknowledge and affirm a job well done, we can also take the next step of letting their supervisor know how much we appreciate them. Building up a DSP by viewing their job as a valuable contribution makes a difference in how they see themselves.

While writing this book, I have come to admire DSPs even more. Direct support professionals, caregivers and nurses are making immense sacrifices to care for others during the COVID-19 pandemic. Thank you for making a difference during such a difficult time in our history.

I provide DSPs tools to be successful with online connections, instructions, and personal Q & A opportunities. Go to sharlenemeakins.com/resource to check out these resources.

Sharlene Meakins, BSN, RN

SHAUNA'S STORY

DSP's make a huge difference in the lives of the people they support. Some of our customers have been through so much, have little to no friends, some have no family, and they have to deal with people treating them badly due to their diagnosis. We step in to help care for daily needs with their dignity intact and figure out the least intrusive way to do this.

DSP's help customers accomplish their goals and dreams. They support them in making new friends and take them out as requested. They have changed my life as well. I have worked as a DSP/Medical Liaison at Sunny Oaks for 20 years. I love coming in and making a difference in the lives of our customers. I do my very best to make them feel valued and care for them the way they choose. This job can be very difficult and demanding at times. To see them smile, to hear them say my name makes it all worth it. When they call me an *old lady* or *grandma* is the best feeling. It definitely makes me smile. I know that I have made a difference at some point in their lives.

It is hard for the customers to trust staff. Sometimes they lose staff so quickly. At times it is difficult to get our customers through medical procedures and such. This is where our DD Nurse comes in handy. She is by our side every step of the way. She is always willing to help, coming up with things to help improve their health/safety. She understands the details with orders and special circumstances that are involved with getting medical care for the DD population. Some of our customers cannot do the standard procedure/test to help figure out the problem or offer a solution.

Shar is amazing and acts with integrity. She is so kind, gentle, and has a heart of gold. She is great at problem-solving and figuring out a way to help. She helps to make sure the customers' wishes regarding their medical care is what the customer wants, not what the staff wants or the doctor wants. She is a great advocate for the DD population. She never talks down to the customers or staff, and no question asked is a stupid question. I don't know what we would do without Shar, our DD Nurse.

Lessons Learned:

- The DSPs in the DD field are truly our heroes.; they make a difference in the lives of those they provide support for every day.
- If someone truly has a heart to support individuals with I/DD, it's not 'just a job' to them; find ways to draw out their strengths and provide him or her with the tools they need to grow.
- When faced with a problem, realize it's not the staff's lack of abilities; look beyond the circumstances and use your problem-solving skills to discover a solution.

Chapter Fifteen

A PAPER TRAIL AND DATA REVIEW

"The goal is to turn data into information, and information into insight."
~ Carly Fiorina

As with any healthcare position, whether a physician, nurse, or caregiver, documentation can be a never-ending and overwhelming task. These are a few things that I have learned over the years and am still learning. As a caregiver or nurse, ensure that you know the policies and procedures of the agency you are working for. The documentation requirements vary from one agency to another. Know the **Nurse's Practice Act** of your state for specific rules and guidelines.

As I shared earlier, a disgruntled family member, after the death of their sibling under my nursing care, reported to the Board of Nursing that I was negligent in their care. My documentation was reviewed and it was determined that I had not been neglectful and their reported complaint was not substantiated. I knew that I had done a good job of documenting and I provided excellent care for this individual. But I experienced some fear and apprehension as a nurse because of being reported. I knew that we had discussed this in nursing school but I didn't think that it would unjustly be done to me. It served as a reminder to use the computer and software tools I had been given to document consistently.

Once again, always ensure your paper trail and instructions are easy to read and understandable for staff. Write professionally with complete sentences and proper language. Documentation is a legal document that can be used in court. They are not text or shorthand notes to your family and friends. We often get into the bad habit of using acronyms that we think everyone knows, i.e. LOA - leave of absence, DX - diagnosis, FX - fracture, the list goes on and on.

The most important component I've learned is to ensure that I and staff complete follow-up information until a concern is resolved with clear statements. If we leave documentation open-ended and do not follow-up as to whether an as-needed prescription was effective or not, it appears once again that we are neglectful in ensuring that the individual is receiving the healthcare and pain relief they need. Proper documentation can make all the difference in a State onsite review of the interpretation of an individual's care.

The benefit of our computers and software today is healthcare tracking being available electronically. As a DD Nurse, you can monitor health tracking without needing to go to the individual's home. You are able to review intake and elimination, hours of sleep, medication administration, vitals, glucose readings, and so on right from your own office. Take full advantage of the software system that is provided to you as a nurse. As a result, you will be closely linked to the direct support professional to review the much-needed information to prevent health concerns of aspiration, constipation, dehydration, seizures, and any other health risk involved. I myself was so glad that I was introduced to Therap Services, LLC, www.therapservices.net, an easy to use computer software specifically designed to support agencies who serve the I/DD Community.

Lessons Learned:

- Take advantage of the State Board of Nursing training for community nursing opportunities to learn where you need to improve.
- Take the time to ensure that the DD Nurse and staff complete follow-up information until a concern or documentation is resolved with clear, grammar-accurate statements.
- Utilize computer software to facilitate easy access to health tracking and the ability to complete health care reviews remotely.

Chapter Sixteen

CONTINUE TO GROW AND INVEST IN YOURSELF

*"Investing in yourself is the best investment you will ever make.
It will not only improve your life, it will improve
the lives of all those around you."
~ Robin Sharma*

As with many careers, it is important to take the time to invest in your academic growth. Some careers require continuing education credits in order to maintain your license. Healthcare services and nursing fall in that category. I was a certified pharmacy technician for six years prior to completing my RN, which required the completion of continuing education with each certification renewal. That was the first job that I had ever had that gave me the understanding of investing in my own academic growth in a field.

It was during that time I was reminded how much I enjoyed learning new skills even though I struggled academically as a younger student. As I look back, I amazingly was not limited by my age. I didn't think that I was not able to learn because I was too old, even though I had five adult children and am a grandmother. Therefore, when I meet men and women who admire my courage to go back to school, I encourage them to pursue their dreams.

Our dreams are not limited by age. When I was first considering going back to school several years ago, someone said to me, "Most people are only in a career for 15 to 20 years, so if you completed your degree in 4 years, how many years do you still have to work in a new career?"

Wow, when I did the calculations, I could easily work as a nurse for 15 to 20 years. So after completing my Associate's Degree in Nursing (ADN), I didn't hesitate to complete my BSN degree online from my living room. The online opportunities are endless in developing our academia in any topic.

Often, the lies that we believe about ourselves are the biggest limiting factors for us investing in our education: *I am not smart enough. I'm too busy. I'll fail my classes. No college will accept me.* And the list goes on. Or, maybe you have people in your life who do not believe in you and they have discouraged you from going back to school as I experienced.

More times than not, I allowed other people's opinions to keep me from doing what I had the desire to do several times throughout my life. Had I completed my nursing degree the first time I was taking my prerequisites, I would have been a nurse 20 years earlier. I believe that our desires are given to us by God and it's never too late. We are born with a purpose and only we know our true heart's desires.

Now that I know that I enjoy and am perfectly fitted to be a DD Nurse, I have purposed to obtain my certification as a developmental disabilities nurse. I am purposeful in studying and preparing for the exam. I want to be a life-long learner, love life and it's the length of days.

Take the time to invest in yourself to be a lifetime learner and pursue your dreams and desires without hesitation. It's only as we move forward that change can be implemented in our lives. What I have come to realize is that many of us have struggled to be all we were meant to be no matter what our lives have entailed.

A Path of Purpose

One such person I respect is a woman who looked beyond her disabilities and was willing to invest in her education and training in order for her to fulfill her purpose. I have had the privilege of supporting this woman as a DD Nurse and we've grown to respect each other and encourage one another in our individual journeys. I would like you to hear from her in her own words her experience with overcoming.

DAWN'S STORY

My name is Dawn. I'm a customer of a DD agency where I also work. I live in one of their 24-hour residential group homes and have known Sharlene Meakins for six years. Ever since I have lived there, Sharlene and I have considered ourselves more than just friends. We are each other's cheerleaders. We encourage one another In our endeavors, including our continued education classes. Sharlene is working on continuing a nurse certification while I am struggling to complete my BS in interdisciplinary studies.

One month after I moved to the group home, I was taking a shower and fell out of my shower chair. I fractured both legs. I don't remember the paramedics or the emergency room ordeal, even though they said I was alert the whole time. What I do remember was being surrounded by hospital personnel trying to turn me over in bed. They hit my leg on the railing and the pain was so excruciating I thought I was going to die. I stayed in the hospital for a week before being transferred to a nursing home, where I stayed for four months.

My mode of transportation is a power wheelchair. I consider myself somewhat independent, but my staff at home didn't feel comfortable taking care of me with two fractured legs. The nursing home didn't handle my care as one would expect and because of that, Sharlene had to intervene several times. In order to keep my legs from bending, they were supported with splints. My orthopedic physician told them I was not to take off my splints. However, the nurse took them off to give me a shower.

I have not stood on my legs for over ten years, so you can imagine my panic when the physical therapist tried to get me to stand. After finding out about this, my sister told them again that I could not stand, which is what we had been trying to explain to him. The physical therapist told my sister that she was not helping the situation. That is when I called Sharlene again. I'm sure glad Sharlene was on my side.

Lessons Learned:

- **Investing in yourself is not about going into debt, but rather view it as increasing your value and what you have to offer.**
- **It's easier to quit than challenge yourself to keep going; too often people give up right at the brink of success!**
- **Look beyond your shortcomings into your strengths to be all you were meant to be.**

Chapter Seventeen

PERCEPTION IS EVERYTHING

"Being disabled should not mean being disqualified from having access to every aspect of life."
~ Emma Thompson

As physicians, nurses, and most caregivers, we've been trained to view providing medical services and care as a means of supporting an individual with I/DD to become "normal." This view can be seen as a form of ableism, defined by Merriam-Webster as *"discrimination or prejudice against individuals with disabilities."*

By seeing a disability as a defect, something to be corrected, those in the medical field with the best of intentions are sending the message that a person with disabilities is inferior to the non-disabled. One result of this is that a person with a disability is often seen through the eyes of others with sympathy and pity. An individual with a disability does not want your pity.

I've often heard someone say about a pregnancy, *I just hope they are born strong and healthy.* What does that mean? Well-meaning people told me that during my own pregnancies. What if my child is born with a disability? Does that mean I will love them any less? If my child is born with 'abnormalities' does that make them any less of a valuable member of my family, our community, or society overall?

Sharlene Meakins, BSN, RN

When I was having my children, testing was just starting to come out to determine if a child had DNA that would indicate if the child had Down Syndrome or other 'birth defects.' As a result of the testing, a mother could decide to terminate the pregnancy based on the results. I couldn't believe it! Why would someone want to terminate a pregnancy due to a test that said there was a birth defect? Besides, the results may not even be accurate!

During that time, as I mentioned previously, I had a son born with birth defects. We were encouraged to do genetic testing. I wasn't sure why the genetic testing was necessary and with four children all under six years of age, driving 120 miles one way for a clinical evaluation more than once was not feasible. Besides, I don't even recall the physician explaining why the testing would be valuable. All I knew was that the love I had for my son would not change. Now that I understand more of the purpose of genetic testing, I would have chosen differently for the sake of my son and his own choices based on his overall health and wellness goals as an adult.

What I have come to realize as a DD Nurse is that not everyone has my perspective. I have been not only grieved but angry at office visits when a physician's comments reflect that a treatment or surgical intervention is not warranted because someone has a disability. They may view a person with a disability as someone who does not have a quality of life or purpose. Are you kidding?!! If that was me at that same appointment, I would be offered all the testing and intervention that I needed.

On the other side of the coin, a physician may begin ordering therapies or treatments that the individual or support team has not requested. For example, in Dawn's story, you see a woman with cerebral palsy who has been in a wheelchair since she was 12 years old, and the physician orders PT so they can begin to walk. Or, you see a speech-language pathologist who recommends a feeding tube because someone has difficulty holding their head up without any indications of choking or aspiration. Richard Riser, Director of Disability Equality in Education describes this as the 'medical model' of disability which sees the disabled person as the problem.

Usually, the focus is on the impairment rather than the needs of the person. As nurses, we must not only look to the medical model to understand how to support individuals with disabilities but the social model as well. Whereas the medical model intends to correct the "mistake" of the disability, the social model says that there is nothing inherently wrong with disability itself, but asks the world to change its ableist perceptions that a disability is a defect and start to view it as an identity in the same way that race, sex, or sexual orientation is viewed.

By seeing disability through a social model, we, as nurses, allow ourselves the opportunity to see the gifts I/DD disabilities can provide. As the story of Dr. Temple Grandin, a famous academic with autism made clear, "...the world needs all kinds of minds." Through her story, we see that by accepting and embracing the gifts the disabled body can provide, and by promoting an environment that allows those gifts to surface without correction, we are promoting a truly inclusive world where people with disabilities can thrive.

As DD Nurses, it's important first of all to ensure that we know what an individual wants, needs, and desires. Secondly, we need to determine if the individual even wants the nurse to serve as an ally who comes alongside them to provide support with their health and wellness goals?

Often as nurses, we come in assuming the role of an advocate who moves in to control and demand that the individual's health and wellness needs are met from their own perspective. This is an ableist perspective, and yet, an easy trap to fall into. I have caught myself on more than one occasion thinking I need to "fix" something that I view as a problem. During those times, I remind myself that I only can provide information to help an individual make an informed decision. I am not responsible for the outcome of an individual's choices.

Don't we see that with our own families? Maybe we have a loved one that we want to quit smoking or stop eating junk food day in and day out? Or even stop resorting to alcohol or drugs to bury their emotional or physical pain?

Sometimes, an individual may need someone to be an advocate and speak up in order to ensure that the healthcare or mental health provider understands what the individual wants or doesn't want. Often, I have found that clinics do not have the proper transfer equipment in order to perform a proper assessment, exam, or testing. Even the exam tables and radiology tables are not equipped with safety measures to event prevent a fall.

Each of us needs to understand that we need to make our own choices. We do not need to be a victim of another's perspective or perception but make an informed decision. We can facilitate the mindset that can help any individual to be successful in their heart's desires, needs, and wants.

How can we think outside the box and implement tools that will make all the difference? For example, I really enjoyed the television show, Speechless with JJ, a nonverbal high school student with cerebral palsy who uses a power wheelchair, a communication board, and had an aide. His success was facilitated with tools that helped him to be independent and to be able to communicate his needs, wants, and desires. This is an example of the second approach defined by Richard Riser as the 'social model' of disability thinking which views the barriers that prevent disabled people from participating in any situation as what disables them.

As described above, the social model asks more about how society can change the environment and their perceptions about disability so that individuals can thrive, rather than expecting the person with a disability to try to fit into a mythical non-disabled norm.

It's essential that we as DD Nurses and those who support an individual with I/DD that we check our perspectives. We each must ask ourselves, "Do I view someone with disabilities as someone who needs to be 'fixed' or do I view everyone as a whole person with needs, wants, desires, and dreams?"

***

Gratefully, I have met physicians and nurses who have an amazing understanding of providing health and mental health care services for an individual. I have found that these rare individuals typically have either had a sibling, family member, or child with disabilities. Or, they worked with several individuals with disabilities at a facility where they practiced. They are definitely the exception.

I was so encouraged by a friend who told me that as a child with disabilities and the many hospitalizations he experienced, he loved the nurses that took time to order food for him that he enjoyed and spending time with him when he was alone. Truly, a nurse with a heart of compassion, acceptance, and kindness can make a difference in a moment.

BLAYNE'S STORY

As a person with a disability which the medical establishment defines as I/DD, I have had many opportunities to interact with those in the medical profession. There was the physical therapist with her strong Swedish accent who came to my school every Tuesday to stretch me, to help me improve my core, and to teach me how to fall safely. And then there was the caregiver I hired after I moved into my first apartment at 19. And the occupational therapist who took the time to ask whether I had sex in my wheelchair when fitting me for a new one because if I did she surmised the arms should raise.

Those professionals I remember most, who made the biggest impact on my life and the success I have become, did not do so by trying to teach me to stand up straight or pick up my foot when I walked. They didn't make a difference by encouraging me to keep walking no matter the cost. They made a difference and an impact by seeing me as a whole person.

That physical therapist in school brought me books. Because of her I read My Side of the Mountain, many of the Roald Dahl books, and ignited my love of reading. When she would go on vacation, she would bring me back little trinkets and tell me about the places she had gone. That caregiver I hired after I moved into my own place took me to my first gay bar, helping me to find community in a part of my life that had been otherwise ignored and overlooked. She took me to sign up for classes at the local community college.

As I reflect on the intent of this book, to help provide well-rounded and practical approaches to nurses and other professionals who provide supports for folks with disabilities, I know one thing for sure: I was able to succeed, to obtain a Masters degree, to live independently, to pull myself out of poverty (all of which are statistically uncommon for people with disabilities) not entirely through my own fortitude, but because of people like Shar.

People who fostered my love of reading. People who showed me the world was so much bigger and had so much more to offer than I could see from my forested rural home far out on the Olympic Peninsula of Washington State. People who honored my whole being, who saw me for me—disability and all—and encouraged me to live authentically, to honor myself, and honor my body and my brain just as it was.

Lessons Learned:

- **Look not only to the medical model but to the social model as well to fully understand how to support individuals with disabilities.**
- **You can make a difference in the lives of others by imparting hope and courage until they can have their own.**
- **Honestly ask yourself -** *Do I view someone with disabilities as someone who needs to be 'fixed' or do I view everyone as a whole person with needs, wants, desires, and dreams?*

Chapter Eighteen

OVERCOMING TRAUMA

*"You treat a disease: You win, you lose. You treat a person,
I guarantee you win - no matter the outcome."*
~ Patch Adams

We have all experienced trauma in our lives at one point or another in some framework or another. Trauma comes in many degrees of emotional, mental, and physical as a result of abuse or neglect. Abuse and neglect are shamefully a huge part of the I/DD Community. Children and adults alike are treated as the 'less than" population. We must as healthcare and mental health care providers, caregivers, family members, and community support staff be aware of the signs and symptoms of abuse and neglect.

The NCADD states that:

> *"...individuals with I/DD are 2.5 to 10 times more likely to experience abuse. Not only once, but repeated abuse... One study estimates that 49 percent of people will experience 10 or more incidents of abuse. Researchers have found that more than 90 percent of people with intellectual disabilities will experience some form of sexual abuse at some time in their lives. They estimate that 15,000 to 19,000 people with I/DD are raped each year in the United States. Most*

> incidences of abuse and neglect for people with I/DD are not reported. This is especially true for people receiving services in congregate settings where up to 85 percent of cases of abuse go unreported. When abuse is reported, most cases do not lead to prosecution or conviction. Almost all abuse is perpetrated by someone that a person with a disability knows; some research estimates up to 96 percent of cases."
>
> Friedlander, Kelly. *"DD Councils Addressing Sexual Abuse and Neglect."* NACDD, Nov. 30, 2017, www.nacdd.org/dd-councils-addressing-sexual-abuse-and-neglect/.

My experience has been that if someone has been sexually abused, they may refuse to allow assistance with their personal hygiene. They often refuse bathing or showering due to their vulnerability. Also, an individual may exhibit self-injurious behavior because they don't want to be touched or change clothing. It's not unusual for someone to sleep on top of their covers fully dressed since they don't want to get into bed due to previous abuse.

There are many circumstances that place an individual with I/DD at risk. Such as the risk of exploitation. A common example of exploitation is when someone hires a person with I/DD for a job and they are only paid pennies to perform the work compared to someone without disabilities.

Independent individuals with I/DD are exceptionally vulnerable in the community. They may purchase furniture, a television, or a telephone at stores where they do not need a line of credit and take the purchase home the same day. As a result, they sign a contract that requires them to make monthly payments with limited income. This is especially concerning for those individuals that do not have employment in the community but only depend on their social security benefits to pay rent, buy groceries, and pay their bills.

Financial abuse is another risk an individual with I/DD often experiences. If they have no concept of the value of money, it makes it difficult for them to make purchases in a store without needed guidance from someone that can be trusted. If an individual is depending on someone else to handle their money, this also places them at significant risk. It's essential that support staff have the character of integrity, which C.S. Lewis defined it as, "Doing the right thing even when no one is watching."

Each member of an individual with I/DD's support team must know the individual and their history in order to understand the risks they face. Discussion among the team also addresses discerning:

- Is the individual at risk of leaving a supervised setting?
- Does the individual abuse alcohol or illegal drugs?
- Does the individual engage in the unsafe use of flammable material or ingest non-edible objects.
- Does the individual refuse medical services, treatments, or medications?
- Does the individual engage in illegal or high-risk sexual behavior?
- Does the individual use weapons or use objects to attempt to harm someone?
- Do they engage in behavior that is harmful to animals?
- Do they participate in unsafe social behavior by interacting with strangers or lack of awareness that puts them at risk when using social media?
- Do they invite people into their residence where they are taken advantage of by "guests" that stay overnight, days at a time?

Again, the value of an individual with I/DD having trusted support is essential with someone who knows the risks and is aware of what to look for evidence of trauma. This is especially true for those who provide daily support for the individual to live a successful and fulfilling life.

The direct support professional must recognize and attempt to prevent events that may trigger those individuals with severe emotional distress or physical reactions to something that reminds them of a traumatic event (which mental health professionals determine as a post-traumatic stress disorder). An attempt to avoid these events would be to avoid thinking or talking about the traumatic event and by avoiding places, activities or people that remind the individual of the traumatic event.

Understandably this requires a significant amount of patience and intervention on the part of the caregiver. A key point for the DSP is that they recognize that this is nothing personal towards them when an individual is triggered and responds in fear, hatred, anger, or even violence. Too often as staff, we take an individual's reaction to heart instead of being aware of the environment and how to make quick interventions to reduce the elevated response in the moment.

Lessons Learned:

- **Know the risks of abuse and be aware of what evidence of trauma to look for; it's essential that an individual with I/DD be able to trust his or her support team.**
- **Each member of his or her support team must know the individual and their history in order to fully understand the risks they face.**
- **Be careful not to take on the role of a parent in order to fix and correct; your place is to come alongside an individual to provide support and to help facilitate good decision making while gaining skills to reach their goals.**

Chapter Nineteen

WELLNESS VS ILLNESS

"Take care of your body. It's the only place you have to live."
~ Jim Rohn

I believe one of the challenges I face as a DD Nurse is to attempt to provide instruction and support to adult individuals in their overall health and wellness. I find it very disheartening that the guidelines for healthcare are dictated by a medical mindset rather than from a prevention mindset. I recognize that it has been improving over the years but the truth is that in the intellectual and developmental disabilities realm, we have a long way to go.

I find that instead of being proactive to prevent illness, we are proactive in treating illness once signs and symptoms surface. For example, instead of having funding for individuals to be provided with good supplemental and nutritional food therapy, they are given laxatives and stool softeners in daily quantities to improve elimination. To help relieve evidence of muscle pain, they are given oral analgesics and narcotics rather than given massage therapy. The list goes on and on.

Our bodies are amazing vessels and yearn to be properly cared for with good nutrition, hydration, exercise, and rest. Most often, I have found that the individuals we support are often addicted to sugar, living on soda, cookies, cakes, cereals, and processed food. My mind screams when I read a meal menu that is filled with boxed and frozen processed foods that are quick and easy but filled with sodium and preservatives. Their diets lack variety with high fiber, nutritious foods that are flavorful, and a joy to eat.

Needless to say, this isn't always the result of those that plan, cook, and prepare the food. If we are honest with ourselves, many of us have resorted to the fast and easy drive-thrus and grab the quick and easy meals on the shelves. I myself have cared for young adults that did not even know how to use silverware because they were raised on fast food.

I believe we can make a difference in the health and wellness of our individuals by being proactive in their care by teaching good alternatives for their daily food and fluid intake. We can further be proactive by suggesting activities that include exercise, fresh air, and positive relationships. I understand when direct support professionals tell me, "...but I offer those things, and they always say no!" The truth is, we need to be an example of someone that is living a healthy lifestyle to encourage someone else to follow in our footsteps.

Obviously, we still need to address illness when it arises but the most effective way to support an individual to have a successful, productive, and happy life requires health and wellness prevention.

One way we as DD Nurses do this is by writing protocols that provide staff with the information they need to keep the individuals within the boundaries of health and safety. These protocols typically have four sections:

Section 1: About this issue - how is the person at risk?

Section 2: Steps to prevent harm - what precautions to carry out.

Section 3: Expected response - signs or symptoms that need to be addressed.

Section 4: When to Call 911.

Four protocols of prevention that are prevalent for individuals with I/DD are aspiration, constipation, dehydration, and seizures.

Often referred to as 'The Fatal Four due to the fact that if any of the signs and symptoms of these four occur without recognition, left undetected can cause death.

Other protocols that are important to write are for any chronic disease such as heart disease, at risk for falls, unreported pain, PICA, and diabetes. Any protocol can be written out in the above format for clear instructions and steps to implement.

Again, it is essential to know the individual you support and their health and wellness risk to ensure that in best practice, illness is prevented and treated when symptoms are recognized.

Lessons Learned:

- **While you need to address illness when it arises, the most effective way to support an individual in having a successful, productive, and happy life is health and wellness prevention.**
- **Making simple, easy changes in the types of foods that are prepared and consumed provides the first step to wellness.**
- **Knowing an individual with I/DD's health risks is imperative in order to write protocols that provide clear, understandable instructions for staff to follow**

Chapter Twenty

HEALTHCARE OUTSIDE THE DD COMMUNITY

*"Service doesn't have to be big and grandiose
to be meaningful and make a difference."*
~ Cheryl A. Esplin

As was true for me, I was never given the "training" I needed to understand the process of recognizing the needs of someone with intellectual or developmental disabilities. What do you do if someone can't communicate with you? What do you do if you don't understand if they are in pain, or their likes and dislikes?

I have found this so true in the clinical and hospital settings. It is essential for individuals to have primary care providers who not only understand their health care needs but who see them as a person. They address the individual personally whether they are verbal or nonverbal.

I have compassion for nurses who have had no experience with individuals whose needs are different from those they usually serve. When I've had individuals I support admitted to the hospital, the nurses are so grateful for the staff and DD Nurse to communicate how an individual completes ADLs. But, it is disturbing when someone with DD funding is placed in a facility that the funding goes to the facility. As a result, this means that the home and/or agency that provides care for the individual who's been admitted to the hospital no longer receives funding to care for their needs. Alas, the individuals that have staff they trust are not funded to support them during their hospitalization or rehabilitation which an agency is unable to afford to provide.

Also, health care providers often don't understand the administrative rules a DD home and/or agency must follow. It can be difficult for orders to be clear and concise for support staff to understand and follow. I've met healthcare staff who think that you can "make" an individual do something that they are unwilling to do, even if it means not taking their medications. As a result, a DD Nurse plays a key role in working with the clinical and hospital RNs, care coordinators, and support professionals to acquire all the individual needs for healing and improving their health.

When an individual has serious health issues, it's often difficult for their home to provide their needed medical care when being discharged from a hospital. Therefore, it's essential that they are stable for staff to support their needs once home. The challenge is, most individuals are uncomfortable outside their homes and do not desire medical support in a long-term care home or rehabilitation center which can be traumatizing. Home Health Services are very helpful but once again, they need the support of the DD Nurse and staff in order to understand the individual's overall needs in order to provide proper care.

One such service that can be challenging is speech and language therapy. An order to eat five small meals a day may not be agreeable to the individual. They are not willing to split their three regular meals into five smaller meals. Or, they may not be willing to allow staff to cut up their food or thicken their fluids.

Physical therapy may also be a challenge when an individual does not want to participate in an exercise program.

Despite the fact that we are doing everything we can to support an individual and improve their health, we may hit obstacles that make it difficult to complete the task as caregivers.

Once again, the much needed trusted support staff is essential in building positive relationships to facilitate a life-giving healthy lifestyle.

Lessons Learned:

- **Despite the fact that you are doing everything you can to support an individual and improve their health, you may still hit obstacles that make it difficult to complete the task as a caregiver.**
- **Be compassionate to nurses who have little to no experience with individuals whose needs are different from those they usually serve.**
- **Staff and DD Nurses are needed to be able to discuss with the individual's healthcare providers the signs and symptoms that they are seeing to obtain the proper diagnosis and treatment.**

Chapter Twenty-One

THE DD NURSE AND THE I/DD PROVIDER

*"Every day you wake you and have a second
chance to do whatever you want,
to be whoever you want. The only thing stopping you is you."
- Jennifer Lopez as Maya in the movie <u>Second Act</u> (2018)*

As I have worked with I/DD providers, I've come to recognize that there are key points that a provider and an RN should discuss. When an agency is in need of a nurse to support one of their individuals, it is imperative that they are a good fit for one another. I know that often an agency contracts with a nurse just because they need a nurse. As a result, both the nurse and the agency can become unhappy with the arrangement.

Often, nurses may have a heart to work for an agency because of a staff member they know or an individual living in one of their homes. This alone does not warrant the ability to serve as a DD Nurse. I've seen nurses take a part-time job to serve as a DD Nurse when their only nursing practice experience has been at a hospital on a medical/surgical unit. They have good observation and assessment skills, but the application of those skills are different within a DD residential or agency setting.

Key Points to Discuss During an Interview:

1. Does the nurse have experience with the I/DD population? Personally? Professionally? Or both?
2. In their most recent employment as a nurse, were they required to complete a full assessment, write a care plan, and write protocols based on the needs of the individual?
3. Are they aware of the Fatal Four Protocols?
4. Do they have experience in training and providing delegation for staff who serve as direct support professionals for individuals with I/DD?
5. Have they worked with a State Department of Health Services previously?
6. Do they believe that they have good working relationships with other health care professionals?
7. Do they believe themselves to be good team players, able to come together to make the best decisions with others for someone with I/DD? (They don't have the last word when it comes to the care of an individual.)
8. Do they approach health care with a holistic view? Body, Soul, and Spirit?
9. Do they recognize the need for partnering with mental health and behavioral providers for proper assessments?
10. Do they understand the role of someone as a guardian or health care representative?

These were key points that I did not understand when I started working as an RN in the DD field of practice. Therefore, I am so grateful that I am seeing more nursing programs and opportunities coming forth to learn more about the DD field prior to serving as a nurse.

I believe that acquiring a DD Nurse mentor is essential. Without DD Nurse mentors and professionals in the field of I/DD, I would have quit. But my confidence grew as I remained teachable and asked questions.

Do you need a DD Nurse mentor in your life? Do you have a passion

A Path of Purpose

for DD Nursing but don't have someone to rub shoulders with to grow in your profession?

Please, consider my "New Developmental Disability Nurse On-Boarding" program. Go to my website: sharlenemeakins.com to contact me for further information and support. I would have never thought years ago that I would enjoy teaching. You never know what's in store for you when you start stepping out of your comfort zone.

***

I would like for you to hear from a physician who I met at a DDNA event several years ago and since that time we've connected at other events. I have admired his years of experience working with nurses in the DD field as well as his training and encouragement of DD Nurses who have a passion for the field. I have utilized his writings and training by purchasing "Clinical Pearls in I/DD Healthcare" and "Curriculum in I/DD Healthcare." Any DD Nurse would benefit from the purchase of these materials.

CRAIG ESCUDÉ, MD, FAAFP, FAADM

After medical school, I began working at a Federally Qualified Health Center (FQHC) providing general family medical care in Mississippi. I heard that the nearby Mississippi State Hospital needed physician coverage in the evening hours, and I began moonlighting there.

While most of the patients that I provided medical care for at the state hospital had significant mental health issues, we had occasional short term admissions of people with intellectual and developmental disabilities from a state program across the highway called Hudspeth Regional Center. Hudspeth was also in need of a physician, and I decided to leave the FQHC and begin working there as well.

I quickly learned that my medical school and residency training did not provide me with the necessary skills and experience to deliver healthcare to people with disabilities. I acquired most of my skills from the nurses and direct support professionals that had been working there for years. It wasn't that the disease conditions were any different, it was that they presented in a different way, with different frequencies and that communication of symptoms was largely non-verbal. I had to learn to understand the language of behavior and how subtle changes in a person's behavior were often the sign of a brewing health condition.

During my clinical career, the move from mass isolated living arrangements to community-based arrangements was progressing. It wasn't difficult to see that as people moved out of facilities they would be receiving their medical care from community-based clinicians, most of whom, like me, received little training in the health needs of people with I/DD.

I made it my mission to do something to improve the availability of clinicians who could meet the needs of people with I/DD. I created a state-wide program called, DETECT, the Developmental Evaluation, Training, and Educational Consultative Team of Mississippi, whose purpose was to educate clinicians about this important, but neglected field of medicine. As more people with disabilities move into community settings from larger facilities, the healthcare network simply **must** become more competent in this field. I believe that anyone with any level of disability should be able to visit any clinic and receive a basic level of competent and compassionate healthcare. Education and experience are the keys to this statement.

I retired from my role as Medical Director of Hudspeth Regional Center in 2018 to become President of Health Risk Screening, Inc. HRS's mission is: *To assist vulnerable persons to achieve a health status and quality of life comparable to that of the population at large.* It could not have aligned better with mine. My work with HRS has connected me with many people in this field throughout the country and the world. That's how I came to know Sharlene. People like Shar are so important to help ensure that those with I/DD receive the healthcare they need.

A Path of Purpose

To work for a company that not only shares but encourages creativity and progress towards better health for people with I/DD is a dream. HRS is the developer and sole provider of the Health Risk Screening Tool (HRST) that not only identifies health risks in people with disabilities but provides action steps to mitigate these risks in a very person-centered way.

In addition to the HRST, HRS also produces high-quality, educational electronic learning courses that educate supporters of all levels about identifying and reducing health risks in people with disabilities. Since coming on board, I've been able to take what I've learned over the years the hard way and create an eLearning course geared specifically toward physicians and nurses. It's called the Curriculum in I/DD Healthcare and it provides the fundamentals of I/DD healthcare to clinicians of all types.

What a journey! You can learn more and see how it continues at HRSTonline.com

Lessons Learned:

- **When an agency is in need of a nurse to support an individual with I/DD, it is imperative that they are a good fit for one another.**
- **Don't take lightly the skills necessary to be a DD Nurse; fully utilize the tools and training available to advance your career.**
- **Reach out for help; you are not meant to learn the lessons alone.**

Final Thoughts

Who would have ever thought that someone challenged me to write a book less than twelve months ago? I started out writing my story just to have an ebook on my website for anyone wanting to get to know me as a DD Nurse. I knew I wanted to make a broader impact on the lives of individuals with intellectual and developmental disabilities by supporting DD Nurses, direct support professionals, agencies, group homes, and families. What I didn't know was how to do that.

Therefore, as I contemplated starting my own DD Nursing contracting business, I hired a business coach in order to help me develop a plan. Natasha and Rich Hazlett, the founders of Unstoppable Influence, www.unstoppableinfluence.com, came alongside me with a passion and desire for me to step out of my comfort zone and into my purpose. Little did I know what was about to unfold.

While attending the author and speaker workshop by Natasha and Rich, I was encouraged to also hire an author coach, Don Hutson, https://donhutson.com/, to ensure that what I had to offer was a book written with value for every reader. As the months went on, Don provided me with tools and ideas on how to get my heart and passion on paper. My desire grew stronger to make a broader difference as I was writing. I realized that I wanted to be a face the DD Community recognized as "a DD Nurse who wanted to Make A Difference Together." That I was there to encourage and support others in their personal journey.

This book has become a wonderful representation of a decade filled with dreams, relationships, purpose, and divine intervention. It was only as I realized that I had a choice to step up and choose what was placed on my heart that I could then move forward and be successful. I have come to learn so many valuable lessons throughout this journey with the anticipation of many more to come.

This book has also become an amazing representation of what it takes to support one another. We each bring valuable pieces of the puzzle to the table which together facilitates moving forward the dreams and desires for each one of our lives as represented by the many stories.

My desire for you, the reader, is to not only begin to recognize your own *Path of Purpose* but to step out in faith and believe that nothing is impossible through Christ who strengthens you.

Acknowledgments

My heart smiles as I think of all the people that are, have been, and will be a part of my life on *My Path of Purpose*. There are so many people to acknowledge and thank that this list is endless. When I think back over the years of my relationships, I realize that each step of the way my Lord has brought amazing people across my path. Nothing is happenstance.

- ★ Thank you to my friends and family members who encouraged me on my journey to becoming an RN. Without your support, sacrifices, and prayers, I would have turned back many times.
- ★ Thank you to the Developmental Disability Nurses Association who has connected me with outstanding DD Nurses in my life and provided much-needed training.

My heartfelt appreciation is extended to everyone that invested in this book:

- ★ Rich and Natasha Hazlett who encouraged me to write a book and believed that I was an Unstoppable Influencer.
- ★ Don Hutson who walked me through the steps of writing a book and helped me recognize the value I had to offer.
- ★ Brain Varley who saw the potential in me as a DD Nurse as a "new" nurse and has offered great value to its content.

- ★ Gretchen Koch who came alongside me and saw the value of this book and the need to reach out to DD Nurses and the I/DD Community.
- ★ Christine Hoy who understood my heart for this book and answered God's call to be my editor.
- ★ Jessica Tookey who provided the beautiful cover painting, Virginia Path. To see more of her wonderful art go to JessicaTookey.com.
- ★ To each and every person and family that contributed the stories to this book that emphasizes the importance of 'Making A Difference Together.' The value of this book shines because of your courage in following your own *Path of Purpose*.

All honor and glory goes to my Heavenly Father
and Lord who has directed my steps in
My Path of Purpose to be who He created me to be!

Glossary

BSN, RN	Bachelor of Science in Nursing, Registered Nurse
CDDN	Certified Developmental Disabilities Nurse
CNA	Certified Nurses Assistant
DD	Developmental Disability
DD Nurse	Developmental Disability Nurse
DDNA	Developmental Disabilities Nurses Association
DSP	Direct Support Professional
HIPAA	Health Insurance Portability and Accountability Act
I/DD	Intellectual and Developmental Disability
ISP	Individual Support Plan
NACDD	National Association of Councils on Developmental Disabilities
OAR	Oregon Administrative Rule (Each State has their own administrative rules.)
ODDS	Oregon Developmental Disability Services
POLST	Physician Orders for Life-Sustaining Treatment
PSW	Professional Support Worker
RC	Residential Coordinator (Each agency has various names for this position.)
RD	Residential Director (Each agency has various names for this position.)
TL	Team Leader (Each agency has various names for this position.)